THE
SHAAR
PRESS

THE JUDAICA IMPRINT
FOR THOUGHTFUL PEOPLE

RABBI ABRAHAM J. TWERSKI, M.D.

DEARER

A
SHAAR
PRESS
PUBLICATION

THAN LIFE

MAKING YOUR LIFE MORE MEANINGFUL

Published by **SHAAR PRESS**
Distributed by MESORAH PUBLICATIONS, LTD.
4401 Second Avenue / Brooklyn, New York 11232 / (718) 921-9000

Distributed in Israel by SIFRIATI / A. GITLER BOOKS
10 Hashomer Street / Bnei Brak 51361

Distributed in Europe by J. LEHMANN HEBREW BOOKSELLERS
20 Cambridge Terrace / Gateshead, Tyne and Wear / England NE8 1RP

Distributed in Australia and New Zealand by GOLDS BOOK & GIFT SHOP
36 William Street / Balaclava 3183, Vic., Australia

Distributed in South Africa by KOLLEL BOOKSHOP
22 Muller Street / Yeoville 2198 / Johannesburg, South Africa

ISBN: 1-57819-179-3 Hard Cover
ISBN: 1-57819-180-**7** Paperback

Printed in the United States of America by Noble Book Press
Custom bound by Sefercraft, Inc. / 4401 Second Avenue / Brooklyn, N.Y. 11232

Table of Contents

DEARER THAN LIFE

Introduction

t is strange how idioms may sometimes develop that convey a concept which is the polar opposite of the literal meaning of the words.

The human being is comprised of two components: body and soul, or in Hebrew, *guf* and *nefesh*. When one sacrifices oneself for a principle, one really is sacrificing the *guf* in order to preserve the integrity of the *nefesh*. Yet, the term for self-sacrifice is *mesiras nefesh*, as though it were the soul that one is surrendering rather than the body!

If we were to take the words literally, there are unfortunately many, many instances of *mesiras nefesh,* where people have abandoned the soul in order to gratify the needs and aspirations of the body. It is *mesiras haguf* that is a rarity. Perhaps if we had better insight into the need of preserving the integrity of the soul, and how this has been done throughout the ages right into our own era, we might begin to give preference to our spiritual needs.

The term *mesiras nefesh* is here to stay, so we will continue to use it, recognizing that we are referring to its symbolic rather than literal meaning. We shall hopefully be able to demonstrate that properly understood, *mesiras nefesh* is within everyone's reach.

Whereas the common usage of *mesiras nefesh* refers to self-sacrifice, there is another concept which is contained in the term if we understand the word *mesirah* to mean "turning over."

A chassid of Rabbi Schneur Zalman was not feeling well, and on one occasion, while sitting with several other chassidim, he said, "The Rebbe is thinking of me now." The chassidim later heard from their friends who had been in Liadi with the Rebbe that indeed, at that precise moment, the Rebbe had said, "Our friend Reb Shmuel is in need of a refuah (healing)."

The chassidim pounced upon Reb Shmuel. "What right have you, an ordinary mortal, to exhibit clairvoyance, as though you had prophetic inspiration?" Reb Shmuel defended himself. "I have no prophetic inspiration. It is just that each time I was at the Rebbe, I turned a part of my soul over to him, so that now my soul is completely in the Rebbe's custody. That is why I was able to feel that the Rebbe was thinking of me."

This is also how a person can "turn over" his entire being to the Divine will, so that he unites and identifies with G-d. There is then no need to "sacrifice" one's will in deference to the Divine will, since the two are one and the same.

There may therefore be some confusion in the text as to precisely which way the term *mesiras nefesh* is being used, and all I can do is apologize to the reader for this multiplicity of meanings.

The subtitle of this book "Making your life more meaningful" implies that there is a need to search for ways to give meaning to life. This may come as a surprise to some people, who may assume that their life already has meaning. A bit of analysis will reveal this may not be true.

Much of Western culture appears to consider happiness as the ultimate goal in life, and defines ideal happiness as freedom from all distress and enjoyment of all pleasures. This is certainly not the Torah concept, which considers human life to be mission oriented, with every person having a reason for his existence and a specific assignment to complete on earth. If being content were all there is to seek in life, then endowing man with the capacity of intelligence was counterproductive. Cows in the pasture are undoubtedly far more content than sophisticated humans. Seeking meaning in merely being content hardly befits an intelligent person.

In order for a person to have self-esteem and a feeling of value, life must have meaning. In fact, meaning and value are inseparable.

"Esteem" comes from the Latin word that means to evaluate or to appraise. Let us look at what is the basis of self-esteem and how we ascribe value to anything.

If we look around at all the objects in our homes, we will find that with the exception of items that have sentimental value only, we value things for one of two reasons: aesthetic or functional. Thus, you may have a handsome grandfather clock whose mechanism has broken and cannot be repaired. You nonetheless keep the clock because it is an attractive piece of furniture and it beautifies your home. However, if your can opener broke, you would undoubtedly get rid of it, because it has no aesthetic value, and since it can no longer serve its purpose it has no value at all.

Let us now apply these criteria to ourselves. There may be a few people who are so attractive that they can consider themselves ornamental, but most of us cannot really think of ourselves as having great aesthetic value. This leaves us only with function as a basis for value, and raises the question: Just what is our function? What purpose do we serve? While the hedonist may, at least temporarily, gratify his physical desires, can he really find purpose in being content? What can the hedonist do when the existential question of finding meaning and purpose in life intrudes itself into his consciousness? Too often his only recourse is to try and distract himself from such thinking, and not infrequently he may render himself oblivious to the tormenting feeling of worthlessness by numbing his mind with substance abuse.

I have learned much from my work treating alcoholics, and I can understand why the prophet reprimands people by comparing them to inebriates: "You are drunk, albeit not with wine; you err, albeit not with ale" (*Isaiah* 29:9). People who deviate from the Divine will and allow their behavior to be determined by gratification of their desires are very much like the alcoholic, who indulges his craving for alcohol, even though it is blatantly self-destructive.

Ironically, the alcoholic has an advantage over a non-alcoholic self-indulgent person, in that the lethal nature of his behavior often becomes so apparent that he recognizes he must take drastic action to save his life. The non-alcoholic self-indulgent person may lack such tangible evidence of his self-destructive behavior. Thus, one of the founders of Alcoholics Anonymous wrote, " We must find a spiritual basis for life, else we die," and many alcoholics who have experienced the consequences of yielding to their drive for drink fully understand him. Several thousand years ago, Moses said, "I have set before you life and good on the one side, and death and evil on the other, and [I tell you to] choose life" (*Deuteronomy* 30:19), yet many people are oblivious to the fact that by neglecting to choose Torah they are condemning themselves to death.

Rabbi Schneur Zalman says that if one fails to implement the *neshamah,* one lives the life of an animal, and yes, it is possible to be sophisticated and still be an animal. If a person does not live a spiritual life, then his spirit is dead, and what remains alive is nothing but the physical, animal-like body.

The Torah-observant person would seem to have risen above prevailing secular hedonism. However, Ramban warns us to be cautious, because it is possible to be technically observant of all Torah precepts and yet miss the point entirely, as one may be "crass (even while remaining) within the confines of Torah law" (*Leviticus* 19:2). The 613 Torah precepts are the building blocks of Torah living, but unless put together properly may remain just that: a pile of blocks, but not a structure. For there to be a structure, Ramban says, one must adopt an attitude of *kedushah* (holiness). This can also be seen in the verse in *Deuteronomy* (13:5), where, after saying "you must follow and fear G–d, observe His mitzvos and hearken to His voice and serve Him," the Torah concludes, "and cleave onto Him." All the preceding must lead to the goal of coming close to and uniting with G–d.

Rabbi Moshe Chaim Luzzato (RaMCHaL), in *The Way of G–d,* explains that the purpose of man's being on earth is to transform himself from an earthy creature to a spiritual entity, and in *The Path of the Just* he outlines 10 steps for achieving the *kedushah* which Ramban cites as the purpose of life, hence that which gives meaning to life.

The transformation from an earthly creature to a spiritual being involves dispensing with types of behavior that are characteristic of earthly creatures, which are essentially driven by impulses that gratify the *guf.* Giving meaning to human life and according it the dignity it deserves therefore requires *mesiras haguf* or, as it is paradoxically more commonly spoken of, *mesiras nefesh.*

Let us now look at some of the ways in which we can give true meaning to life, by achieving the transformation of which RaMChaL speaks.

The Heritage of
the Patriarchs

esiras nefesh — literally opting to surrender one's life rather than violate the Divine will — is a concept which represents the highest degree of spiritual devotion to G-d of which a person is capable. According to *halachah,* forfeiting one's life is required in only three instances: if one is threatened with death unless one commits murder, adultery, or idolatry. In all other cases the concept of *pekuach nefesh* prevails; i.e., that when one's life is in danger, all Torah restrictions are suspended until the threat to life has passed. Hence, in the event of a life-threatening condition, one is required to do whatever is necessary on Shabbos to preserve life, and one is required to eat on Yom Kippur if a doctor has established that fasting would endanger the patient's life.

Unfortunately, Jewish history is replete with instances of martyrdom. During the many and varied episodes of persecution, when the only way to survive was to renounce the Jewish faith, countless Jews surrendered their lives rather than deny their G-d. Outstanding among these is the account of Hannah and her seven sons, all of whom chose death rather than bowing to an idol, and even when the cruel monarch was unable to tolerate the consequences of his edict and said to the seventh son, "Do not force me to kill you. I will throw a coin to the ground and you will bend down to pick it up, and in this way it will appear as though you had made obeisance to the idol," the son refused to give even an illusion of concession, and accepted martyrdom. Many similar instances of heroism are recorded in the history of the Inquisition, when Jews approached the auto-da-fe proclaiming *Shema Yisrael* with their last breath. A contemporary of that period, Yaavetz, describes that many unlearned Jews, some of whom had not even been totally observant of Torah, accepted martyrdom rather than deny G-d.

My father used to explain the episode of Moses' vision of the burning bush in this way. The thorn bush, barren of leaves and fruit, represents a person who is devoid of knowledge of Torah and mitzvos. Yet, this barren thorn bush was burning with fire, indicating that within even a barren person there is a passionate flame of faith. Moses said, "I must go see this wondrous sight." G-d then said to him, "I am the G-d of Abraham, Isaac, and Jacob." In other words, within every Jew, learned or unlearned, observant or non-observant, there exists the nucleus of a passionate adhesion and devotion to G-d, a heritage of the Patriarchs to their descendants and to their spiritual descendants who sincerely adopt Judaism, and when threatened to be separated from his G-d, this spark of devotion bursts into a passionate flame (*Exodus* 3:1-6).

While the *mesiras nefesh* of martyrdom may be seen as the supreme act of self-sacrifice, there is another type of *mesiras nefesh* which may even surpass this. After all, death is but a momentary occurrence, following which one joins in the incomparable bliss of being in the Divine presence. There is a *mesiras nefesh* of life, where one continues to sacrifice and accept ongoing suffering. This is pointed out in the introduction to the *Midrash* on the Book of *Lamentations*.

When Jerusalem fell to the Babylonians, and the survivors of the massacre were exiled from their homeland, the Patriarchs came before G-d, pleading for mercy for the Israelites. Abraham said, "I waited so long for a child, and when I finally had Isaac at the age of 100, I loved him dearly. Yet, when You told me to offer my beloved son to You as a sacrifice, and all my dreams of having an heir to whom I could bequeath my knowledge of You evaporated, I did not hesitate to do Your will. Will You not recall this and have mercy on my children?" G-d did not respond to Abraham.

The Patriarch Isaac then approached the heavenly throne. "I was a grown man of 37 when my father told me he was going to sacrifice me. I could have resisted, but out of my devotion to You I told my father to bind me tightly to the altar, lest I be overcome at the last moment by the will to live. I gladly gave my life to You. Will You not recall this and have mercy on my children?" Again, no response from G-d.

Jacob then said, "I suffered for two decades from my father-in-law, Laban, and I was relentlessly persecuted by my brother Esau. I bore all my distress with equanimity, only to fulfill Your will to establish the twelve tribes and guard them as a hen does her eggs. I suffered so much in raising them! And now, will You not remember this to have compassion on my children?" Again, no response.

Moses then pleaded with G-d. Moses, whose interces-
sion for the sinful Israelites in the desert was never turned
away, said, "For 40 years I carried Your children on my
back, like a beast of burden. When they angered You, I re-
peatedly offered myself as a sacrifice to attain forgiveness
for them. When I finally brought them to the Promised
Land and You decreed that I could not set foot in the land
of my dreams, I accepted my death as Your will." Yet G-d's
only response was, "This is My decree!"

The Matriarch Rachel then arose and said to G-d, "You
know how much Jacob loved me. I knew that my father
was a scoundrel, and would likely substitute my sister
Leah in my place. I therefore gave Jacob a secret pass-
word, so that if Leah were to take my place at the
wedding, he could discover and expose the ruse. When
my father did indeed put Leah in my place, I realized that
if Jacob asked for the secret password, my sister would be
publicly humiliated, and I therefore told Leah the secret...
I, a mere mortal, was ready to surrender the man I had
hoped to wed and allow him to become my sister's hus-
band. All this, just to spare my sister a few moments of
humiliation. You, Eternal King, must You wreak
vengeance against the false gods [which the Jews worship
in Your stead], by exiling my children and allowing them
to be massacred?"

G-d responded to Rachel, " Dry your tears, My child. It
is in your merit, Rachel, that your children will be returned
to their land" (Pesichta to Eichah Rabbah).

How strange! The pleas of Moses and the Patriarchs are not
even acknowledged. It is only Rachel whose words arouse the
Divine compassion. Why?

The *mesiras nefesh* of Moses and the Patriarchs was indeed
great, and even today we invoke the devotion of Abraham,
Isaac, and Jacob in our daily supplications. But the Divine

wrath was so intense that even the supreme *mesiras nefesh* of surrendering one's life could not appease it. The *mesiras nefesh* of Rachel, however, was of a different order. She did not accept death, but rather the interminable distress of living in deprivation and suffering. And for what purpose? To spare her sister a brief moment of humiliation. This kind of *mesiras nefesh* surpasses even that of martyrdom.

The virtue of Rachel's *mesiras nefesh* was particularly great because it was to prevent someone from being publicly humiliated. It is of interest that although this is not one of the 365 Scriptural prohibitions, the transgression of embarrassing someone publicly is so severe that it causes one to forfeit one's share in the World to Come, even erasing the accumulated virtues of a lifetime of Torah study and performance of mitzvos (*Ethics of the Fathers* 3:15). Rachel's refinement of character was such that it was actually easier for her to accept a lifetime of deprivation than see her sister put to shame. Rachel anticipated the Talmudic dictum, "It should be easier for a person to throw himself into a fiery furnace than to publicly humiliate someone" (*Berachos* 43).

Rachel transmitted her spirituality to her son. The Torah states that when Joseph could no longer contain himself and revealed his identity to his brothers, he called for everyone to vacate the room, and no one outside the immediate family was present at the disclosure. Rashi comments that he did not want anyone to witness his brothers' embarrassment at the substantiation of their selling him into slavery (*Genesis* 45:1). The *Midrash* states that Joseph put himself at great risk, because in absence of outsiders, the brothers might have killed him. Yet Joseph reasoned, "I would rather be killed than humiliate my brothers before the Egyptians" (*Midrash Tanchuma Vayigash*). In Torah literature, Joseph is referred to as "the *tzaddik*," not only because of his moral integrity, but also because of this sensitivity. In kabbalistic literature, the trait of *yesod* (foundation) is ascribed to Joseph, again, not only because moral purity is the foundation of Judaism, but also because preserving human dignity is fundamental to Judaism.

We refer to Rachel as "our mother," although the majority of Israel are descendants of Leah. While Rachel is the biological mother of only two tribes, she is the spiritual mother of all of Israel, to which anyone who has poured out their hearts and shed tears at her tomb can attest.

We are fortunate that we are not often called upon to accept martyrdom, but there are abundant opportunities when we can have the *mesiras nefesh* of Rachel. And just as Yaavetz noted in his time, we may find examples of this type of *mesiras nefesh* even in people who are unlearned, and even among those who may lack a total commitment to Torah observance. As my father indicated in his discourse on the burning thorn bush, it is the nucleus of spirituality bequeathed unto us by Abraham, Isaac, and Jacob that lives eternally within us, and gives us the capacity to rise to dazzling spiritual heights.

I recall my father referring to a man as a "true tzaddik." Sam was a man whose knowledge did not exceed reading the siddur. During the depression years of the 1930s, one was fortunate to have any kind of job. Furthermore, those were the days when the workweek was at least six days, and Sam could not retain a job because he would not work on Shabbos. He had no reason to believe that things would improve, and his decision to observe Shabbos essentially meant that he was relegating himself to poverty, earning whatever he could at odd jobs in order to feed and clothe his family. Sam did not even consider this to be mesiras nefesh. Working on Shabbos did not warrant a second thought.

Several years ago I helped establish a treatment program in Israel for ex-convicts whose criminal behavior

to support their drug habits had resulted in repeated imprisonment.

One of those who came seeking help was Avi, a man of 34, who had spent half his life behind bars. After Avi completed treatment he took a low paying job. One day the administrator of the treatment facility received a call from a family whose elderly mother had passed away. They wished to donate her furniture to the center. Annette, the administrator, called Avi for help, and he borrowed a truck to transport the furniture. As he dragged an old, worn-out sofa up the stairs of the center, an envelope containing 5,000 shekels fell from the cushions. This was ownerless money, and the rule of "finders-keepers" could easily have been invoked. Instead, Avi, who had once stolen purses for as little as 10 shekels, gave the money to Annette to buy some new furniture for the center.

Avi was barely supporting himself, and the 5,000 shekels could have helped him live more comfortably for a long time. Avi's turning over the money was a *living mesiras nefesh*.

Sam was a simple person; Avi, a man with a lengthy criminal record. Whence came their *mesiras nefesh?* As my father said, a heritage from the Patriarchs, Abraham, Isaac, and Jacob. This nucleus of devotion is present within all of us, sometimes only in potential, lying dormant, awaiting the opportunity to be manifested.

Let us look at some examples of *living mesiras nefesh*, as we find it in the great personalities of our people, as well as in the Sams and Avis. This may help us discover the nucleus within ourselves, which we may then more easily activate.

What Can Be Dearer Than Life?

T he drive for survival is instinctive in all living things. How can anything supersede this powerful drive and cause someone to forfeit his life?

The answer is simple. People who suffer from severe, unrelenting pain and do not see any relief in sight may well choose to die rather than to continue to suffer. Obviously, the tolerance for pain varies considerably from person to person, but the basic principle is probably valid for all.

Physical pain is not the only mode of suffering that may be intolerable. As children studying American history, we were impressed by the declaration of Patrick Henry, a hero of the American Revolution, who declared his refusal to remain under the dominance of a foreign power. "I know not what course others may take, but as for me, give me liberty or give me death."

The prospect of living a life of coerced servitude and being deprived of the right to steer one's own course in life can render life meaningless and undesirable.

Torah teaches us that the essence of human life is "to cleave unto G-d" (*Deuteronomy* 30:20). This can be achieved only through observance of the Divine will as expressed in the Torah. Anything which threatens to separate a person from G-d threatens to deprive one of the very essence of life. Indeed, we find this concept in the ecstatic expression of the Talmudic sage, Rabbi Tarfon, who said to his colleague and teacher, Rabbi Akiva, "Separation from you is like separation from life itself."

It is a principle of Torah, however, that preservation of life overrides all Torah ordinances, with the exception of the three cardinal sins: adultery, idolatry, and murder. In all other instances, the principle of *pekuach nefesh* prevails, whereby the Torah requires doing whatever is necessary to preserve life.

In absence of a physical threat to life, the choices a person makes ultimately will depend on his system of values. The more spiritual the person, the more devoted he is to the principles of Torah. When confronted with a choice between violating the Torah and sustaining personal loss or discomfort, he will choose that which is for him the lesser of the evils. Thus, the Matriarch Rachel had achieved so lofty a level of spirituality that the prospect of seeing her sister humiliated publicly, albeit for a brief moment, was more painful to her than even surrendering the man she hoped to wed.

Mesiras nefesh thus becomes a question of values. Actually, all behavior is a question of values. The Talmud states, "Calculate the loss of a mitzvah as compared to its gain" (*Ethics of the Fathers* 2:1). Thus, if a person neglects a mitzvah because it will cause him a loss of several dollars, he is setting a value for that particular mitzvah, that he does not consider it worth more than that sum. We might apply this principle to the common practice of rushing through the morning *davening* at breakneck speed in order to get to the office or the place of business a few minutes earlier. Doing this puts a dollar value on *davening.*

Without exception a person will invariably choose whatever constitutes the least discomfort. Spiritual development consists of making the fulfillment of the Divine will the prime motivation for living, and the violation of the Divine will the greatest suffering.

This principle is eloquently stated by Rabbi Dessler in his essay on *bechirah* (freedom of choice). Rabbi Dessler points out that for every person there are actions that are unthinkable and do not require a struggle to choose.

For example, someone who has been reared since infancy in observance of the highest standard of *kashrus* is not even tempted in the least to eat *treifah.* Even if extremely hungry, this person may pass a non-kosher fast food outlet which exudes an aroma of tasty food, and will not give the slightest consideration to partaking of the *treifah* food. The idea is so absurd that he does not even contemplate it and does not have to struggle to suppress an impulse to eat. Furthermore, he does not consider this to be a sacrifice. To the contrary, eating *treifah* is so abhorrent that to do so would inflict a degree of suffering far worse than feeling hunger.

It is possible, Rabbi Dessler says, that this person might not have the same resistance to other Torah prohibitions. For example, he might not be completely averse to listening to a juicy piece of gossip, which constitutes a violation of the Torah prohibition of *lashon hara,* either spreading or accepting gossip. When confronted by someone who wishes to share gossip, this person may have to struggle to walk away or terminate the conversation. In other words, for him *lashon hara* is not in the same category as *treifah,* and his further spiritual development requires making *lashon hara* as much off limits as eating *treifah.*

Thus, Rabbi Dessler says, *bechirah* is a matter of a frontier, and spiritual development requires advancing the frontier so that more and more issues, those that are incompatible with

Torah, are relegated to a state of being unthinkable, which would no longer require exercising conscious restraint and struggling to suppress temptation, because the latter would no longer exist.

So it is with *mesiras nefesh.* A person who has newly adopted observance of kosher observance may have to exert conscious restraint to avoid satiating intense hunger with non-kosher food, and if he does this, this is a measure of *mesiras nefesh,* whereas for someone for whom *treifah* is an abomination, this avoidance is not a *mesiras nefesh.*

We can see that *mesiras nefesh* may not be in the committing or the avoidance of specific behavior, but rather in the exercising of spiritual growth and development to advance the frontier of *bechirah.* Thus, Sam's *mesiras nefesh* consisted of making Shabbos so sacred and inviolable that the question of working on Shabbos was never an issue.

For the Matriarch Rachel it was the avoidance of causing humiliation for her sister; *l'havdil,* for Patrick Henry it was liberty; and for Sam it was Shabbos. For Avi, who applied the Rambam's teaching that in order to eliminate an undesirable character trait one must overcorrect, the renunciation of his criminal past made the retention of unearned money unacceptable. For everyone there are principles that are so vital to one's existence that their violation is so intolerable as to make life itself intolerable. It has been aptly said that if there is nothing worth dying for, then there is nothing worth living for. It is the concept of *mesiras nefesh* that is so unique to man, and that sets him apart qualitatively from all other forms of life.

Yes, there are things that are dearer than life. This is generally true of all people. It is only a question of what those things are.

My father used to tell a story about two people in his hometown, Hornostipol. My great-grandfather, the Rebbe of Hornostipol, had as his shamash (aide) a man by the name of Dan, who had been a boyhood friend, and lat-

er became attached to the Rebbe, and virtually never left his side. The official town rabbi was a man by the name of Yankel. After the Rebbe died, Dan and Yankel both laid claim to the cemetery plot adjacent to the Rebbe. Yankel claimed that as the official rabbi of the village, his claim had priority. Dan claimed that inasmuch as he had virtually never left the Rebbe's side during his lifetime, he deserved to be near him after death. They brought their dispute before my grandfather, who suggested that they leave the matter in the hands of G-d; namely, whoever would die first would be buried next to the Rebbe.

My father related that if Dan became sick, Yankel would organize fervent prayers for Dan's recovery, and bring in the finest medical treatment available, for fear that Dan might die and precede him to the coveted grave. Similarly if Yankel became sick, Dan would act likewise. Each one was hoping that he would die first.

I am certain that Dan and Yankel both had the normal survival instinct. Yet, there was something that was clearly dearer than life.

As human beings, we all have desires, and only angels are free of any desires. But what our desires are may indicate what kind of human beings we are.

Only One Will

We have alluded to the concept that *mesiras nefesh* is not perceived necessarily as a sacrifice. The Talmud instructs us, "Negate your will before G-d's will, and make His will your own" (*Ethics of the Fathers* 2:4). People of great spiritual achievement did indeed adopt the Divine will as their own, hence what appears to us to have been a supreme sacrifice was not at all a sacrifice for them. They were merely following their own will, as all of us do. It is just that their own will had been transformed to be the will of G-d.

The Talmud states that the Patriarchs observed the mitzvos of the Torah hundreds of years before the Torah was given to Moses. How could they possibly have known what the Torah required before it was revealed?

The chassidic writings explain that we do not need instructions to do that which is a natural drive or impulse. No one has to tell us to drink when thirsty, to eat when hungry, or to sleep when exhausted. These are natural bodily cravings which we implement automatically.

The spirituality of the Patriarchs and their devotion to G-d was of so lofty a degree that their will became identified with the Divine will, whatever that would be. Hence, just as we do not have to receive instructions to drink when thirsty, so did the Patriarch Abraham have no need to be instructed to act in a way that constituted fulfillment of the mitzvos. His will, more so, his very instinct was that of the Divine will.

In our prayers we frequently invoke the merit of the Patriarch Abraham whose devotion to G-d was so great that he was willing to sacrifice his only child if that were the will of G-d. This is cited as the outstanding example of *mesiras nefesh* in Jewish history. Many commentaries reflect on the fact that unfortunately Jewish history has abundant examples of martyrdom, some of which seemed to be at least as great as that of the Patriarch. Why, then, is Abraham singled out?

One Torah commentary provides a valuable insight. In relating the episode of the *Akeidah* (Abraham's binding Isaac to the altar), the Torah states that after receiving the Divine command, *Abraham arose early in the morning.* If he awoke, this means that he slept during the night. Just think of it! An elderly father who longed all his life for a child, and was finally given a child at age 100, is now asked to sacrifice that child to G-d. Granted that because of his intense devotion to G-d, Abraham agreed to do so, but how is it possible for a father to sleep peacefully during the night, knowing that in the morning he must offer his son as a sacrifice? Yet, Abraham's sleep was not disturbed even by the awesomeness of the event of the following day. Why? Because for Abraham nothing existed other than the Divine will. He was able to accept everything with equanimity, as long as he knew that this is what G-d wanted. If G-d wished him to have a child, so be it. If G-d wished to take the child from him, so be it. His own feelings were not part of the equation, because there were no "own" feelings. He had perfected what the Talmud teaches, to identify one's own will so absolutely with G-d's that the two became indistinguishable.

In our prayers we often mention the devotion of Abraham, but this is not primarily to remind G-d of the event. G-d hardly needs to be reminded of anything. We do so in order to make ourselves aware of the spiritual heights a human being can attain. Even if we cannot aspire to achieve so absolute an identity of our own will with G-d's as did the Patriarch, we at least need not deceive ourselves that we are but pawns in the hands of our biological drives as some philosophers and some psychologists might have us believe.

Another commentary provides us with a further insight into the greatness of the Patriarch. As the *Midrash* tells us, Abraham was raised in a pagan culture, and indeed, his father was a merchant of idols. At a young age, Abraham realized the fallacy of idol worship, and came to the knowledge of the one true G-d. He then began preaching monotheism, and condemning pagan practices, many of which were frankly barbaric, such as that of human sacrifice. Wherever he went, Abraham riled against human sacrifice, preaching to people that G-d would never demand the taking of a human life as a mode of service to Him.

After decades of preaching his understanding of the Divine will, Abraham is commanded by G-d to offer his only son as a sacrifice, and he prepared to do so. But how would he then face those people whose practice he had so vehemently condemned? Abraham was now 137, and for 100 years he had been admonishing people that their concept of Divine worship was grossly erroneous. He would now have to admit that he had been in error, and that they were indeed right.

Just think of how difficult it is for a person to admit he was wrong, even if it concerns only an insignificant issue. What an immense amount of courage it would take for a person to publicly declare, "I have been wrong my entire lifetime. I retract everything I have ever said. You were right, and I was wrong." There are probably few people in the history of mankind who have been able to so efface themselves.

The Torah relates that Esau sold the birthright to Jacob for a pot of lentils, and that "he ate and drank, arose and left, and Esau belittled the birthright" (*Genesis* 25:34). At a later time, Esau complained bitterly that Jacob had stolen his birthright (ibid. 27:36). At this time, however, Esau could not afford to consider the true value of the birthright, because he had just sold it for a pittance. In order to defend his behavior, he had to ridicule and belittle the birthright as being worthless.

It is certainly not uncommon for people to defend their behavior and rationalize in order to justify their actions. Rather than to admit they were wrong, they will come up with ingenious reasons to avoid admitting a mistake.

This was the greatness of Abraham. He was able to overcome this enormous assault on his ego and was prepared to admit publicly that all his arguments against human sacrifice had been fallacious, and that some of the principles he preached were wrong. The offering of Isaac as a sacrifice would be one kind of *mesiras nefesh*, that of martyrdom. The public declaration, "I have been wrong. I retract everything I preached against human sacrifice," was a *living mesiras nefesh*. Of course, G-d ultimately called upon Abraham not to sacrifice Isaac, vindicating his beliefs.

Ibn Ezra gives us an important insight into the mechanism of transforming one's will. Commenting on the last of the Ten Commandments, "You shall not covet," Ibn Ezra asks, How is it possible to legislate an emotion? One can command another to act or to refrain from acting, since actions are under voluntary control, but feelings are spontaneous. If I happen to see something belonging to someone else and I wish I could have that object, how can I be instructed not to desire it, not to wish it was mine?

Ibn Ezra makes an exceedingly important psychological observation: A person will not covet something that is absolutely beyond his reach. For example, if a person who was enormously greedy were told that on a planet in a distant galaxy many trillions of miles away there are mountains of gold and diamonds, his desire to avail himself of these riches would not be in the least stimulated because there is simply no way he could ever reach them. If a person does feel a strong desire for something belonging to another person, it is only because somewhere in his mind, conscious or unconscious, there lurks a thought that he might somehow acquire it. Therefore, says, Ibn Ezra, if a person were absolutely and totally committed to observance of the commandments "You shall not kill; you shall not commit adultery, you shall not steal," and these were as completely beyond the realm of even remote possibility as reaching a planet many trillions of miles away, the thought of acquiring the object would be such an absurdity that his desire for it would not be aroused in the least (*Exodus* 20:14).

A thorough understanding of Ibn Ezra gives us a different perspective of the 10th commandment. "You shall not covet" becomes a statement of fact rather than an actual commandment. In other words, if one has made an absolute commitment to observance of the preceding commandments, it is then a natural consequence that one will not covet.

We can thus understand the mechanism of transforming one's will, and we can have a better grasp of the principle stated by Rabbi Shneur Zalman in *Tanya*, that "the intellect can dominate the emotions." If one exercises the intellect and has an absolute cognitive acceptance of the Divine will, the proper emotions will follow.

Negating one's own will and accepting the will of G-d as the only driving force in life is not a single, momentary act. Many times during the course of each day our body may make its desires felt. Some of these, as we shall see, require a rechanneling and can find expression in the Divine service, whereas others must be rejected because they are contrary to the Divine will. Hence, acceptance of the will of G-d must be repeated not only daily throughout life, but many times each day. This is why, much like the devotion of Rachel, it may require a *living mesiras nefesh*.

The Heartfelt Truth

The psalmist lists the virtues whereby a person can merit being in the Divine Presence, and among these is "He speaks the truth in his heart" (Psalms 15:2).

The Talmud explains this trait as that characterized by Rabbi Safra, who was approached by a customer who wished to make a purchase from him and offered a certain sum Rabbi Safra was reciting the Shema at the time, and could not interrupt to respond to the customer. The latter interpreted Rabbi Safra's silence as a rejection of his offer, and increased the amount substantially. This and subsequent ever increasing offers met with silence, and when Rabbi Safra finally concluded the Shema, he said, "I will sell you the item for the amount you offered at first, because in my heart I had accepted it, but I was just unable to respond at the time."

But why is this a virtue? Why would it be unethical to accept the greater sum? Had Rabbi Safra actually demanded a higher price, the customer would have paid it. Since the item was obviously worth the higher price to the buyer, why did Rabbi Safra's unspoken acquiescence to the lesser amount bind him even morally?

Maharsha explains this with the principle of votive pledges. The *halachah* is that if a person makes a silent pledge to donate to the Sanctuary, he is morally bound to honor it. Why? Because since G–d knows a person's innermost thoughts, there is no difference to G–d between a verbalized or a non-verbalized idea. It is only man who requires the spoken word to reveal a thought, because we cannot read another's mind.

Rabbi Safra had reached a level of spirituality where he was in constant communion with G–d. When he gave silent assent to the customer's initial offer, it was as though he had said aloud to G–d, "I am accepting this man's offer." To have then accepted the greater sum would have been reneging on his word to G–d.

Like most of the Talmudic sages, Rabbi Safra undoubtedly lived very frugally, and could certainly have used the extra money which had been legitimately offered him. His refusal to accept the larger sum was probably a significant deprivation and hence a major sacrifice for him.

Or was it really? It is hardly a sacrifice to honor one's word. Yes, it was a *mesiras nefesh*, but not a sacrifice. For you see, Rabbi Safra had so turned his being over to G–d that his thought was equivalent to the spoken word. The greatness of Rabbi Safra lay not so much in his rejecting the larger offer as in having achieved a level of spirituality where thought and word were identical.

"Speaking the truth in one's heart" has application to all of us who may be far from Rabbi Safra's level of spirituality. Our ethical works speak of three levels of human behavior: thought, word, and deed. We are cautioned not to be deceptive, not to dissimulate and act in a manner that is not in keeping with our thoughts and feelings.

It is not uncommon, however, for people to conceal their true feelings, and to act toward others as if they were their bosom friends, whereas in fact they may soundly despise them. Machiavellian duplicity is often practiced in politics, where the smile and hand shake are ingenuous. But even in oral social relations, we may convey misleading messages, wishing to have others believe that we feel much more positively toward them than is actually the case.

The practice of such duplicity may so permeate our being that the borderline between truth and falsehood becomes blurred, and we may begin to believe our own lies. This is not only a moral breach of honesty, but can also result in self-defeating behavior, as our inability to distinguish truth from falsehood leads to our distorting our perception of reality. "Speaking the truth in one's heart," as Rabbi Safra did, may cost a few dollars, but allows us to have a wholeness of character and a moral integrity which can permit a much healthier adjustment to reality.

The Talmud relates that a relative of Rabbi Yannai went from door to door begging for alms. Rabbi Yannai was perplexed. "Your father was very wealthy," he said. "Surely he must have left you an inheritance."

"I have nothing of my father's wealth," the man said.

"Your father had entrusted me with a large sum of money for safekeeping," Rabbi Yannai said. "This is really yours, and you will have no need to beg for alms."

The man shook his head. "I regret to state that my father was not honest in his dealings, and I do not wish to benefit from money that was not earned honestly. Give that money to the public charity. I will continue to ask for alms until I can earn my livelihood."

Rabbi Yannai was impressed. "We are suffering a severe drought," he said. "Pray for us for rain. If you reject your father's wealth because you feel it was not acquired honestly, you have reached a level of spirituality that will merit your prayers being answered."

There is no indication that this man was a person of great learning, yet he had reached a level of ethical integrity that he preferred to humble himself to beg rather than to live in comfort with wealth which he suspected had not been legitimately acquired.

Speaking the truth in one's heart means operating on a single rather than a double standard. Some people have one set of rules governing their own behavior, yet apply another set of rules to other people. We may sometimes be oblivious that we are doing this, because our personal desires may so influence our judgment that we may actually believe we are operating according to a uniform code of ethics. Solomon says, "All a person's ways are just in his own eyes" (*Proverbs* 16:2). The only way to avoid this pitfall is to obtain an opinion from someone who can be more objective.

The chassidic master, Rabbi Meir of Premishlan, lived in dire poverty. One time a couple came to him for a blessing to have children, and a year later Rabbi Meir received a large sum of money along with a letter of gratitude, addressed to "The Great Tzaddik Rabbi Meir," and thanking him profusely for his blessing, since they were now the happy parents of a newborn child. Rabbi Meir's family were thrilled that they would have adequate money with which to buy adequate food and clothing, but Rabbi Meir was very reluctant to use the money. "First of all, this is addressed to 'The Great Tzaddik Rabbi Meir,' and that is not me. I am not a tzaddik. Secondly, the money was sent on the assumption that it was my prayers that were effective in their having a child. I do not believe that my prayers are that potent. Hence, this gift was sent on false premises, and I may not use it."

The family, who knew the great piety of Rabbi Meir, insisted that he consult a halachic authority. A beis din (a rabbinical tribunal) was assembled, and they ruled that Rabbi Meir might legitimately use the money.

Rabbi Meir's conscience was not appeased even by this ruling, and he brought the matter to his wife's attention. She remarked, "Is it not your principle that when a question arises concerning some food as to whether it is kosher or not, you avoid eating it even if the halachic ruling is that it is indeed kosher? You have set a standard that if there has been the slightest suspicion that something may not be kosher, you do not use it even when there is a favorable halachic decision. Why are you abandoning your principle now? Once you have raised the question that this money may not be legitimately yours, the ruling of the beis din to the contrary should not suffice."

Rabbi Meir promptly returned the money to the senders, and continued to struggle to provide bread for his family. He was grateful to his wife for having saved him from the grievous error of abandoning his ethical standards.

How far can a person go to implement absolute truth?

*R*abbi David Luria was the victim of a plot to discredit him by accusing him of treason to the Czarist government. One time, as he stood before the judges, he heard them beginning to speak to each other in French, to prevent his understanding what they wished to discuss in secret. Rabbi Luria, however, was fluent in French, and he distanced himself to the far end of the room. When the judges asked him why he had moved away, he responded in fluent French, "It was evident to me that you wished to discuss

something with each other that you did not wish me to un-
derstand. However, I could not avoid overhearing you, and
since I do know French, it would be dishonest for me to give
the impression that I am oblivious to your conversation."

Many people think of themselves as being truthful, even absolutely so. They may consider hedging the facts or telling "white lies" as not being an infringement on truth. The fact is that adhering to the truth is far from simple, and requires a *living mesiras nefesh.*

Mesiras nefesh is necessary not only to adhere to the truth, but also to be ever on the alert for the possibility that one may not be totally honest and not be aware of this. RaMCHaL in *The Path of the Just* cites "watchfulness" as being a necessary trait for spirituality, and this requires a person to be on guard for self-deception and failing to recognize that we are less than absolutely truthful.

*I*n Minsk there was a scholar, Rabbi Baruch, who once *pressed a claim against someone who owed him money. At the din Torah (rabbinical trial), the rabbi ruled that inasmuch as there were no witnesses to support the claim, the defendant should take an oath and swear that he does not owe the money. The defendant proceeded to do so. Rabbi Baruch, upon hearing the defendant utter G–d's Name in vain as he swore falsely, could not contain himself and exclaimed, "Rasha (wicked person)! For the gain of money you take G–d's Name in vain!"*

Several years went by, and one day Rabbi Baruch appeared at the defendant's home, asking his forgiveness. "You are asking me to forgive you?" the man said. "You know that I cheated you out of your money."

"Yes, I know," Rabbi Baruch said. "However, this week I was involved in a litigation as a witness. Inasmuch as I was only one witness, the rabbi ruled that the defendant could

go free if he took an oath to contradict my testimony, which he did. This time, too, I could not contain myself, and again I reprimanded him for swearing falsely. However, I did not shout at him with the same force that I did at you, which made me realize that I was more enraged when the false oath was to my detriment. I now realize that my motivation at condemning you was not purely in outrage over defiling the Divine Name, but there was also a selfish motive. To publicly condemn you for taking G–d's Name in vain is appropriate, but to do so for selfish reasons is not. I am here to ask your forgiveness for the intensity of my outburst."

These accounts of the extremism in pursuit of truth may seem to be beyond the reach of the average person, but unless we have a concept of the highest standards, we may not have any guidelines as to what is demanded of us. Perhaps we cannot be as meticulous in self-examination as Rabbi Baruch, but at least we have a concept of perfection so that we can know that we are imperfect.

That truthfulness should supersede all other considerations is pointed out by Rabbi Chaim Shmulevitz, who cites the Biblical account where Moses reprimanded Aaron for not partaking of the sacrificial offering on the day his two sons died. Aaron suggested that perhaps Moses was in error in conveying the Divine command that the High Priest must eat of the offering even when in mourning, and Moses admitted that Aaron was right (*Leviticus* 10:16-20). The *Midrash* states that Moses said, "You are right. G–d indeed instructed me otherwise, but I forgot it."

Rabbi Shmulevitz points out that Moses was in a dilemma. The only avenue for G–d's instructions to come down to us was through Moses. If Moses could forget or be inaccurate, how could we be certain that everything else he conveyed to us as being the Divine will was accurate? Admitting that he forgot would cast suspicion on the validity of everything in the Torah, and place the authenticity of Torah under suspicion throughout eternity. Would it not be better, in this case, for Moses to insist that Aaron was wrong and that his instructions to him were indeed what G–d had said? For the sake of preserving the Torah throughout eternity, it would certainly be more expedient to do so, and Moses could easily have rationalized why he should not admit his error.

This is where we see Moses' devotion to the truth, says Rabbi Shmulevitz. Moses decided that his obligation was not to deviate from the truth for any reason, regardless of what the consequence may be. "It is not my responsibility to preserve the Torah for generations. That is G–d's concern. My duty is to be truthful at all times, come what may" (*Sichos Mussar* 5731:11).

When we justify a "white lie" and rationalize why we are doing so, we would be well advised to think of the standard of truthfulness as exemplified by Moses.

Torah Is Not to Be Exploited

The Talmud exhorts us to study Torah in the purest spirit, and not to use Torah as a vehicle for personal gain. There is much discussion as to how a rabbi or teacher may be accorded his wage, since technically he is not permitted to accept money for teaching Torah.

The Talmudic scholar, Rabbi Yaakov of Lisa, had yet another understanding of the prohibition to profit from Torah. Rabbi Yaakov had received a dowry upon his marriage, and he invested this money with a merchant, hoping to support himself from the income, which would allow him to devote himself completely to the study of Torah without any distraction. Unfortunately, the merchant's business failed, and not wishing to cause Rabbi

Yaakov to interrupt his Torah study, he returned the entire sum to him. *Rabbi Yaakov subsequently found out that others who had invested with this merchant had received little or no money, and he realized that he had been treated more favorably because he was a Torah scholar. This meant that he was profiting from his study of Torah. He therefore gave the money to the beis din (rabbinical court) to be distributed among all who had lost their investments with this merchant. Rabbi Yaakov was no longer able to remain a full-time Torah student, and he then accepted a position as a community rabbi. The burdens of caring for the community's needs distracted him from the full-time study of Torah, something which he valued more than anything else in life, but he felt this was preferable to profiting from Torah.*

There were great Torah scholars who refused to take advantage of their Torah knowledge, and followed the Talmudic dictum, "It is better to strip animal hides in the marketplace than to say 'I am deserving because I am a Torah scholar' " (*Pesachim* 113b). Just several decades ago the renowned scholar, Rabbi Menachem Ziemba, was the proprietor of a hardware store. No one knew of his great Torah scholarship until the Rabbi of Gur disclosed his brilliance and told him it was now his duty to share his knowledge with the world.

In Jerusalem there was a milkman who was once engaged in a Torah discussion for hours with the great luminary, Rabbi Aaron Kotler. Rabbi Kotler exclaimed, "If this is your milkman, then who is your rabbi?"

It is not only Torah knowledge that should not be exploited. Nothing that pertains to Torah and mitzvos should be exploited for personal gain.

*O*ne man, who was a descendant of the great chassidic masters, came to a Rebbe, asking for financial help, and boasted of his ancestry, believing that because he was *of such illustrious lineage, he was deserving of help. The Rebbe told him the following story.*

During the early settlement of Eretz Yisrael, one of the residents found himself in dire circumstances and went to Europe, hoping to raise enough funds from the Jewish communities there to be able to establish himself in some kind of business venture in the Holy Land. However, he never revealed that he was from Eretz Yisrael, because he felt that to do so would be exploiting the holiness for his personal gain.

When the man came to the Rabbi of Rizhin, the latter gave him some money and told him that without fail he must visit Rabbi Meir of Premishlan. When he came to Premishlan, he lodged at an inn.

That day, Rabbi Meir called in his shamash (assistant) and said, "I detect an element of the holiness of Eretz Yisrael. Go to the various inns and see if there is not a traveler who comes from there."

Eventually the shammash discovered the resident from Eretz Yisrael and brought him to the Rabbi, who said, "No one can keep secrets from Meir. I know you are from the Holy Land. Why have you been concealing it?" The man responded that although he was in need of help, he did not feel it was proper to exploit the holiness of his homeland for his advantage.

Rabbi Meir said, "Not long ago someone gave me a large sum of money for tzedakah with specific instructions that it is to be used for helping the needy in Eretz Yisrael." The man was reluctant to accept this money, and did so grudgingly at the insistence of Rabbi Meir, who said that this was his obligation to convey the tzedakah money to someone from the Holy Land.

"So you see," the Rebbe said, "this man was in dire need of help, yet had the mesiras nefesh to restrain himself from telling people that he was from Eretz Yisrael, which

would certainly have facilitated his getting the necessary help. Similarly, you should not exploit the greatness of your ancestors for your personal gain."

The drive for recognition and being acknowledged is very powerful, and is one of the major psychological motivating factors. For a person who can lay claim to greatness to suppress his achievements and knowledge requires considerable fortitude. The humility achieved by some of our great Torah personalities testifies to their *mesiras nefesh* in this regard.

Rabbi Yisrael of Salant, the father of the *mussar* movement and one of the foremost Jewish ethicists, describes the utter humility of his teacher, Rabbi Yosef Zundel.

Rabbi Yosef worked at a trade and repeatedly refused offers of prominent rabbinical positions, feeling that this would be an exploitation of his Torah scholarship for personal advancement. Rabbi Yosef dressed in simple garb, not that characteristic of a rabbi, and was frequently mistaken for an ordinary lay person. One time he was standing near the well when a woman mistook him to be the water carrier, and asked him to fetch several buckets of water for her. Rabbi Yosef did her bidding, and when she offered to pay him he suggested that she pay him the next time. When she later discovered that her water carrier was none other that the renowned scholar, she begged his forgiveness. Rabbi Yosef smiled and thanked her for the opportunity to perform a mitzvah of fetching water for her.

When the Maggid of Koznitz was a child of seven he would return to the yeshivah at night to learn with his friends. On the first night of Chanukah, his father refused to allow him to return at night because it

was customary for the young boys to play games instead of learning. Inasmuch as there was no source of illumination in their house, the child pleaded with his father to allow him to go to the yeshivah, promising to stay only as long as the candle the shamash (sexton) provided would last.

Miraculously, the candle burned much longer than expected, and the child did not return home until the wee hours of the morning. His father, assuming that the child had been playing games with his friends, gave him a sound beating. When the father later discovered that his child had indeed been studying, he asked him, "Why did you let me beat you? Didn't you think I would believe you?"

The child responded, "I knew you would believe me, but is it proper to exploit the study of Torah to escape a beating?"

One of the most outstanding examples of *mesiras nefesh* that I can think of is that of Rabbi Yitzchak Meir of Gur, whose writings testify to his incomparable Torah scholarship.

Rabbi Yitzchak Meir labored long to write a brilliant commentary on the volume of Shulchan Aruch (Code of Jewish Law) which deals with laws of commerce, damages, and other fiscal matters. When he finished this masterpiece, he submitted it for approval to Rabbi Mendel of Kotzk, who had been his colleague, but whom he had adopted as his spiritual mentor.

Rabbi Mendel reviewed the manuscript and then said, "This is indeed a work of genius. However, its very strength is its fault. You see, the accepted commentary on this volume of Shulchan Aruch is that of the Shach (Rabbi Shabsi HaKohen). Your work is so lucid that it would obscure the Shach, who was a great tzaddik and was Divinely inspired.

People may abandon the study of the Shach in favor of your commentary, and that is not proper. I therefore suggest that you do not publish this." And then, pointing to the fire that was ablaze in the nearby fireplace, Rabbi Mendel suggested, "Perhaps it would be best if you destroyed it."

Rabbi Yitzchak Meir did not hesitate. He said softly, "I am hereby performing the mitzvah of the Torah to obey the instructions of the Torah authorities." He then took the manuscript, the fruit of years of labor, and threw it into the flames.

I know that some will disagree with this scenario, and I, too, shuddered when I heard it. But that is not the point. The moral of the story is that it represents a *living mesiras nefesh*.

The Observance
of Shemittah

There is yet another indication that *living mesiras nefesh* surpasses even that of martyrdom. In the event that a person is unable to accept martyrdom when challenged with the commitment of one of the three cardinal sins, and eventually succumbs, say, to commitment of idolatry under duress, he is not guilty of the sin of idolatry, because he did so under threat of being killed. Rather, he has failed to sanctify G-d's Name by accepting martyrdom, which is a much less severe transgression. However, if one fails to accept a *living mesiras nefesh,* the consequences may be more grave.

The Torah requires that every seventh year farmers in Eretz Yisrael must allow their land to lie fallow. This is the mitzvah of *shemittah,* which requires total abandonment of one's land for that year: no plowing, no sowing, no reaping. All fruits of the trees and all vegetation that grows spontaneously is public rather than private property. Anyone may enter a farm or orchard and help themselves to its produce.

It requires great strength of character to forgo an entire year's crops and allow one's farm to lie fallow, and it requires enormous strength of character to watch people wandering through your property, helping themselves to the produce of your land as though it was theirs. But if a person fails to withstand this ordeal, and if he works the land or retains ownership of its produce during *shemittah,* the punishment is most severe for both the individual transgressor and for an entire nation if it violates *shemittah.* Indeed, the Torah states that the reason for Israel being exiled from its homeland is its failure to observe *shemittah (Leviticus* 26:34). Even failure to have *mesiras nefesh* and submitting to idolatry under duress does not have such harsh consequences, but failure to accept the *living mesiras nefesh* is treated far more severely.

The *Midrash* has the highest praise for those who observe *shemittah,* stating that whereas it is relatively easier for a person to subdue his temptation for a brief period of time, the ability to abandon one's land for an entire year is virtually superhuman, and it compares those who observe *shemittah* to heavenly angels. Yet this mitzvah was not assigned only to people who had achieved a high level of spirituality through Torah scholarship and intense devotion. The mitzvah of *shemittah* was incumbent on every Jew, simple as well as learned. We can only conclude that the Torah considers every person to be capable of the strength of character and spiritual fortitude that one might expect only of angels.

Shemittah is the ultimate expression of an unfaltering faith in G-d. The Torah exhorts us not to think that the successes we achieve are the result of our own skill and cunning (*Deuteronomy* 8:17), but to realize that although we are required to do something to earn our livelihood, it is the Divine blessing that determines what the fruits of our labors will be. That blessing will be forthcoming when we live according to the will of G-d, and our livelihood will not suffer from refraining to work on Shabbos, nor from not working our fields during *shemittah*. Actualizing this faith and trust constitutes a *living mesiras nefesh*.

Like the Blazing Sun

RaMCHaL, in his epochal work, *Path of the Just*, states that there is nothing sweeter than taking revenge, and this is something we can all confirm from personal experience. How gratifying it is to be able to give someone his just deserts! But alas! The Torah has forbidden it. Not only does the Torah forbid taking actual revenge, it also forbids expressing a grudge. If someone who has been offensive to you or denied you a favor is now in need of your help, you may not say, "Look here, I am not a scoundrel like you. You refused to help me when I was in need, but I am a better person, and I will help you even though you do not deserve it" (see *Leviticus* 19:18). Rather, you must help that person and keep silent.

Parenthetically, this mitzvah is actually of tremendous benefit. If you cannot take revenge, and cannot express a grudge, of what use is it to hold on to resentments? They can never be acted on, and harboring resentments can therefore never go beyond personal distress. If I cannot act out my resentments in any way, then hanging on to them and allowing them to fester can only be harmful to me, and never toward the offender. Chronic anger has been implicated in a number of diseases, such as high blood pressure, migraine headaches, and digestive disorders. It has been said, "Harboring resentments is allowing someone whom you don't like to live inside your head rent-free." There is certainly no logic in my being tormented because someone else acted improperly.

It cannot be denied that the urge to act out one's resentments is extremely strong, yet the Torah requires us to exercise restraint. The Talmud states that one who suppresses his urge to act out his resentments is "one who truly loves G-d, and can be compared to the brightness of the blazing sun" (*Shabbos* 88b).

His reward is very great, for he thereby merits that his sins are forgiven, just as he is willing to forgive the offenses of others (*Rosh Hashanah* 17a). To suppress one's urge for revenge is a *living mesiras nefesh*.

Clinically, I have come across many incidents where people are unable to divest themselves of guilt feelings. It is true that healthy guilt can be constructive, because it is the distress of the guilt feelings that motivates a person to do *teshuvah* and to make amends for his wrongdoings. There is, however, a pathological type of guilt, which occurs when a person feels guilty for no valid reason, or when a person has done adequate *teshuvah,* yet does not feel forgiven. Inasmuch as the prophet says, "I have wiped away your sins like a fog that has cleared" (*Isaiah* 44:22), which means that when a person has done *teshuvah* his sins are completely erased, just as there is no remnant of a fog after it has cleared, there is no reason for a person to continue to harbor unwarranted guilt feelings, particularly since these can be very depressing and can impair his functioning. The question is: Why are some people unable to accept forgiveness?

The answer is rather simple. We have a true understanding only of concepts with which we have had personal experience. Thus, while we use terms such as "infinity" or "eternity," these are really quite meaningless words, since we have never encountered anything that was limitless or that had no beginning or end. Consequently, although we use these terms, we really have no grasp of what they really mean.

Much the same is true of forgiveness. This may be a term which is as meaningless as infinity or eternity unless we have some personal experience with it, and the only way we can do this is by totally forgiving those who have offended us. When we have done so in a manner that not a trace of resentment remains, "like a fog that has cleared," that is when we can truly understand forgiveness and accept it. It is then and only then that we can shed the unwarranted guilt feelings that can be so destructive. While it takes much effort to accomplish such forgiveness, and this is indeed a kind of *living mesiras nefesh*, the reward of feeling the relief of guilt is great.

O*ne of the luminaries in Jewish history is the "Ger Tzedek of Vilna," the Count Pototzky, who converted to Judaism. Because of his prominent social status, his conversion was a threat to the Church, and he was condemned to death. He fled and lived in secrecy in a village in Lithuania, where he devoted himself to the study of Torah.*

In this village there was a young man who used to torment the Count and disturbed his studies, and when he once rebuked the young man, the latter complained to his father, who came to his son's rescue by revealing to the Church authorities that Pototzky was hiding out in their village. He was arrested, and the death sentence was carried out with his being burned at the stake.

The Church authorities pleaded with Pototzky to recant his conversion, but he was adamant in his refusal. As they brought him to the stake, one of them said derisively , "And I suppose that you are thinking that in the next world you will take your revenge!"

Pototzky replied, "When I was a small child I made little soldiers out of clay. Some of the children crushed my little soldiers, and I was very hurt. I complained to my father, expecting him to punish them, but he simply ignored me. I remember thinking, 'Just wait until I grow up. Then I will get back at these ruffians.' However, when I grew up I realized how trivial this juvenile behavior was, and I simply dismissed it.

"Do you really think," Pototzky said to his persecutors, " that once I am in the eternal world I will accord any significance to this puny, little physical body that you are destroying? To the contrary, I will exert whatever influence I have to achieve forgiveness for the man who turned me over to you, because although his intentions were hostile, he enabled me to fulfill the great mitzvah of mesiras nefesh, by offering my life to exalt G-d's Name.

The *ger tzedek* exemplified both types of *mesiras nefesh*: actual martyrdom, and suppressing an urge for revenge.

This mitzvah is immediately followed by the words, "And you shall love another as yourself," which the Talmud states is the primary principle that encompasses the entire Torah (*Jerusalem Talmud, Nedarim* 9). It is apparent that to fulfill the all-important mitzvah of love for others, one must first triumph over the temptation to seek revenge. Furthermore, inasmuch as the Baal Shem Tov said that the only way one can achieve love for G-d is by love for one's neighbor, the mitzvah of *ve'ahavta*, to love G-d to the degree that one would surrender one's life for Him, is also dependent on suppressing the desire for revenge.

Just as *sinas chinam*, (baseless hatred), disliking a person for no reason, was the cause of destruction of the Temple and the departure of the Divine Presence from Eretz Yisrael, so is *ahavas Yisrael*, the love of another person, the key to restoring His Presence with us.

There is a story of a man who was sentenced to death for alleged treason, and he pleaded with the king to be allowed to go home to put his affairs in order, pay off his debts, etc. The king said this was impossible, because he would obviously use this opportunity to escape, whereupon a friend came forth and offered himself as a guarantee, that he would take his place in jail, and that if the prisoner would not return at the required date, he would be executed in his stead.

When the date for the execution arrived, the prisoner had not yet returned, and the friend was taken to the gallows. Just as the hanging was about to take place, the prisoner arrived and breathlessly ran to the gallows. However, the friend insisted that they execute him instead. "Life without my friend would be meaningless," he said. The word got around to the king that the execution was not carried through because these two were arguing, each wishing to be the one to die.

The king called both men before him and said, "Anyone capable of such devotion, who would not take the opportunity to save his own life, could not have committed the crime of which he was accused." The king pardoned the prisoner, and asked for the two men to accept him as their friend. "I would be honored to participate in such a friendship."

Similarly, when we relate to each other with devotion and *mesiras nefesh*, G-d forgives all our sins and brings His Presence to us, wishing to be included in so wonderful a friend-ship.

It may indeed take much effort to avoid the "sweets" and re-strain our desire to retaliate, but if this merits Divine forgiveness and invites G-d's Presence, it is well worth the price. The *Arizal* said that of all the ways there are to do *teshuvah*, nothing equals keeping one's silence and not retaliating when offended. This is far superior to even profuse fasting.

Rabbi Chaim ben Attar (the *Ohr HaChaim*) related that he once heard a brazen man insult a Torah scholar. He interceded with this scholar and asked him to forgive the man's impudence. "Of course I forgave him," the scholar said. "I did so immediate-ly. You see, the *Zohar* says that when Jews sin, G-d is distressed. If I were not to forgive him, he would bear his sin, and that would cause distress for G-d. By forgiving him, I alleviated G-d of some measure of distress. How could I do otherwise?"

W*hen Rabbi Levi Yitzchak of Berditchev was rabbi in Pinsk, he had many opponents who opposed him bitterly. One time, when he was away from the city, these people took the rabbi's wife and children, put them on a wagon that was used for hauling trash, and sent them out of town. When Rabbi Levi Yitzchak's colleagues heard of this unspeakable atrocity, they appealed to Rabbi Mendel of Vitebsk to pray that the perpetrators of this deed be se-verely punished. "How can I do that?" Rabbi Mendel asked. "Rabbi Levi Yitzchak is standing before the aron kodesh (holy ark) with his Tehillim, praying that no harm befall them."*

We have noted earlier that a *living mesiras nefesh* carries its own reward. This is equally true when we free ourselves of har-boring resentments and grudges.

There is a physiologic reaction which occurs when a person feels threatened. Numerous changes occur within the body to prepare an individual for either fighting off his attacker or flee-ing from him, and these changes, which are automatic, put the body in optimum condition for "fight" or "flight." Among these changes are an increase in heart rate, elevation of the blood pressure, a shift of blood from the digestive tract to the muscles, a shift of blood away from the body surface (pallor), a dis-charge of sugar from the liver into the blood stream, and an increase in respiration. Certain hormones, especially adrenalin, are secreted. These changes are indeed appropriate for optimal coping with a physical attack. They are of relatively brief dura-tion, since the person either successfully escapes from the attacker or the attack is brought to a quick end with either par-ticipant overpowering the other.

This is not so when the attack is of an emotional nature, such as an insult. This type of an attack does not come to an end within a few moments if the victim continues to feel offended. The body reacts to a verbal attack just as it would to a physical assault, with all the changes that were listed above, but if the emotion incident to the insult persists, many of the changes may linger on. It can readily be seen how persistence of these physiologic changes can initiate or aggravate heart disease, high blood pressure, migraine headaches, digestive diseases, skin diseases, or respiratory diseases. If one can overcome re-sentments and forgive an insult, one removes a severe stress from the body, and helps avoid serious diseases. We may think that when we forgive an insult we are being magnanimous. In actuality we are only protecting our own health and life. Thus, far from forfeiting one's life, *living mesiras nefesh* preserves life.

*D*uring the Six Day War, people had crowded into the air-raid shelter of the Mirrer Yeshivah in Jerusalem and were fervently reciting Tehillim as they heard the explo-sions of bombs nearby (the yeshivah was located near the then Jordanian-Israeli border). Among the group was a woman whose husband had abandoned her years earlier *and had left her penniless. The hum of the Tehillim was suddenly interrupted by the cry of this woman: "Master of the universe! I wholeheartedly forgive my husband for all the pain, suffering, and humiliation that he caused me all these years...Just as I have forgiven him, so I ask you to forgive all the sins of those assembled here!"*

Rabbi Chaim Shmulevitz was among those in the shelter and he said, "I don't know if the Tehillim was sufficient to spare our lives. I believe we were protected from the exploding bombs by the virtue of this woman's forgiving her husband's cruelty. We are alive today by her merit."

We are comprised of a physical body and a *neshamah* (soul), which is part of G-d Himself. Spiritually, we are therefore all one, since G-d is absolute Oneness. We are separate beings by virtue of our physical bodies. When we set the latter aside, by a *living mesiras nefesh* which, as we noted, is really *mesiras haguf*, we then remove the barrier and fuse into one being.

It has been asked, "How can the Torah require that we love another person as much as we do ourselves? Is it realistic to demand something which appears impossible?" The answer lies in the first half of this verse: "Do not seek revenge, do not harbor a grudge, and love your neighbor as you do yourself." To the degree that we can divest ourselves of resentments, to that degree we allow our *neshamah* to fuse with those of others. Inasmuch as the *neshamah* is the true "self," we and our neighbor become one, and self-love becomes inseparable from love of others.

The *Midrash* states that a human being can rise to such dazzling spiritual heights that G-d takes great pride in pointing out to the heavenly angels, "Just look at the creature that I have created!" Rabbi Shimshon of Zivlin was such an exquisite person.

When Rabbi Shimshon took the position in Zivlin, he made two stipulations: (1) No communal decision was to be taken without his approval, and (2) the only time he could be consulted was Motzaei Shabbos. The rest of the week he was not to be interrupted from his Torah studies.

The wages of the rabbis in the villages were very meager, and were often supplemented by the rabbi's wife having the exclusive franchise for distribution of yeast in the village. Needless to say, both sources of income did not bring the rabbi's family above the poverty level.

One time Rabbi Shimshon's wife wished to buy a large fish, but the wife of the town's leading citizen offered the merchant a larger sum than the rebbetzin could afford and was given the fish. When the rabbi's wife pointed out that it was really unethical to overbid her, the other woman made a very insulting comment, hurling an obscene invective at her. The news quickly spread around town that this woman had brazenly insulted the rebbetzin, and the townfolk wished to take disciplinary action against her. However, they were restricted from doing so without first consulting the rabbi, and he would not be available until after Shabbos. In order to facilitate getting the rabbi's approval, the townfolk asked the rebbetzin to mention the incident to her husband so that he would be apprised of it by the time they came for his approval.

Friday night, when Rabbi Shimshon returned from shul, he found the Shabbos table set as usual, but his wife had placed a setting for herself in the kitchen. When he inquired why she had done so, she said, "I don't deserve to be a rebbetzin and to sit at your side. After all, the wife of the town's leading citizen told me I was thus and thus," repeating the insulting name she had called her, and that the townfolk were outraged and wished to discipline her but were waiting for the rabbi's approval. Rabbi Shimshon calmed her and prevailed upon her to join him at the Shabbos table.

Just as he was about to recite Kiddush, Rabbi Shimshon asked his wife, "When did this incident occur?" "On Tuesday," she said. "And you mean to say that since Tuesday you have been harboring a grudge against this woman?" the rabbi said. "How are we to begin the holy Shabbos with a heart full of hatred?"

The rebbetzin was taken aback and said, " You are right. I forgive her."

"That is not enough" the rabbi said. "You have been harboring a grudge for four days. It is not enough that you forgive her now. You must apologize to her for having carried this grudge so long," whereupon the rabbi put down the kiddush cup, and accompanied his wife to the home of the woman.

When the family of the town's prominent citizen saw the rabbi and his wife at the door, they were fearful that the rabbi had come to pronounce a curse upon them, and they began weeping, "Please forgive us for the grave sin we have done." Rabbi Shimshon said, "We have nothing to forgive," and turning to the woman he said, "We have come to ask your forgiveness for having harbored a grudge against you all these days." Both parties cried, each asking the other's forgiveness, until they finally embraced in an attitude of true peace and love. Only then did Rabbi Shimshon and his wife return home to make Kiddush and welcome the angels of peace that attend the Friday night meal.

Little wonder that G-d takes pride in His magnificent creation!

Unsung Heroes

There are numerous incidents of living *mesiras nefesh*, all of which indicate a deep conviction of the truth of Moses' statement, "I have set before you today the life and the good (on the one hand), and the death and the evil (on the other)" (*Deuteronomy* 30:15). When we accept the principle that Torah is life and that deviation from Torah is death, there is little wonder why one will choose observance of Torah at all costs. We are certainly not surprised that people will go to the greatest extremes to preserve life, and that is precisely what the person does with *mesiras nefesh*. Furthermore, just as we will take many precautions to prevent a possibly fatal injury or illness, so will we take similar precautions to prevent what we consider spiritual death.

Moshe Aaron was not a scholar. He was a simple, pious Jew, who made an honest, frugal living as a shoemaker. In his community there was but one *mikveh,* and when the *mikveh* was closed for repairs and it was evident that there would be significant delay before it became operational again, Moshe Aaron moved to another town, and did not return until the *mikveh* was again functional.

It is of interest that not all of Moshe Aaron's descendants are fully observant, but even some of those that are not have nevertheless been faithful in the observance of *mikveh.* Why? Because this was a *mitzveh* which had been practiced with *mesiras nefesh,* and it was thereby ingrained in the family tradition. The family had transmitted the concept that to violate the mitzvah of *mikveh* was similar to placing oneself in grave physical danger, which every reasonable person would avoid.

When there is a danger to life, we know that the Torah requires doing whatever is necessary to preserve life. All Torah restrictions are abrogated, with the exception of idolatry, adultery, and murder. But when the threat to life has passed, the Torah requirements are reinstituted.

This gave rise to a dilemma for a very pious Jew who was in the Russian army, and was placed on sentry duty. This required his being stationed outdoors in the sub-zero weather. He was concerned that the coat he was given contained *shaatnez,* a mixture of linen and wool which is forbidden by the Torah, hence he did not put it on. When he felt that exposure to the frigid weather was becoming life threatening, he put the coat on, because at this point, the Torah requirement was to preserve his life. When he felt he had warmed up sufficiently and was no longer in any danger, he removed the coat. Over a 12-hour period of standing guard, he repeatedly put on the coat and took it off, as he calculated just what constituted the Divine will at any particular moment.

Perhaps this may seem a bit far fetched, but think of a person who has a serious heart condition, who is given a strict regimen of what he must do to remain alive and well. One would hardly think of him being fanatic if he adhered faithfully and rigorously to the doctor's instructions. Protecting one's spiritual health should be no different.

Respecting one's parents is a mitzvah the highest order, and the Talmud lavishly praises Dama ben Nesina for his *mesiras nefesh.* The caretakers of the Temple were in need of a particular gem for the breastplate of the High Priest, and they offered Dama a huge amount of money for this precious stone. However, the key to the vault where the stone was stored was under the pillow upon which Dama's father was sleeping. Rather than awaken his father to get the key, Dama forewent the profit which the sale would have brought him. The following year, he was rewarded by having a *parah adumah,* the rare red cow needed for purification, born into his herd.

One does not have to go back in history to find examples of *living mesiras nefesh.* Yonah is a highly skilled teacher, who was given an opportunity to augment his income by taking on a second teaching position. Although he could have fit this into his schedule, he turned down the offer because another young man in the community was in need of a job, and Yonah felt that if he recommended this person, they would hire him. The temptation to increase his earnings was indeed strong, but was overridden by the Torah verse, "And your brother shall live (along) with you" (*Leviticus* 25:36), which Yonah understood to mean that one should not try to gain everything in sight for oneself when another person may be in need.

Perhaps Yonah had heard the story about the Chafetz Chaim, who kept his store open only until he had earned enough for the expenses of that day, then closed the shop so that customers would patronize other merchants. That the Chafetz Chaim had this degree of trust in G-d is hardly surprising. That someone like Yonah, an average person, could develop this level of spirituality makes me envious.

In the community where I grew up there was a man who could hardly read the siddur fluently, and was generally considered to be a boor. One day he became aware that his son had leased a place, where he would buy scrap metal and paper from peddlers, which was located on the same block where there was already an established shop selling these goods. He called his son and told him that in no way was he to open the shop in such close proximity to a competitor. When the son protested that he had signed a lease and was legally liable for the rent for the next two years, the father said, "I don't care if you are legally liable for life! If you open a shop on the same block, I will break your bones."

Every father wishes his children to prosper. This man's sense of propriety and *"menschlichkeit"* took priority over his paternal feelings, and that is a living *mesiras nefesh*.

The mitzvah of *hachnassas orchim*, hospitality to guests, was performed with *mesiras nefesh* by the Patriarch Abraham. The Torah states that at age 100, three days after circumcision, weak and in pain, he sat on his doorstep in the torrid heat, seeking wayfarers whom he might provide with food and lodging.

The quality of mesiras nefesh invested in this mitzvah was later exemplified by Rabbi Meir of Tiktin, who could not sit down to eat a meal unless he could share it with a guest, and he was always looking for strangers in the community who might need a place to eat. One day he could not find anyone whom he could invite, and he ended up fasting that day. He had no intention of fasting, but having habituated himself to sharing a meal with someone in need of food, he simply could not eat alone.

Just as we do not consider it a sacrifice if we do not eat because we have no appetite for food, so Rabbi Meir's fasting was not a sacrifice to him. His mesiras nefesh consisted not in his abstaining from food, but in developing his spirituality so that he was simply unable to eat without sharing the food with someone in need.

There is a type of *living mesiras nefesh* which does approach martyrdom. It is possible for a person to reach a state of devotion to G-d so intense that his *neshamah* (soul) attaches itself to G-d in a manner that causes it to leave the body. The Talmud speaks about the death of Moses and other great *tzaddikim* as coming about by "a Divine kiss." In this case, G-d attaches Himself to the person's *neshamah* in such a way that it cannot reenter the body, with the initiative for this joining coming from G-d. In other cases, the initiative for the joining comes from the person. Some commentaries explain the death of the two children of Aaron (*Leviticus* 10:1-2) as having occurred in this manner.

*R*abbi Uri of Strelisk would bid farewell to his family each morning before going to the synagogue, because he felt that he might expire in his devotion during prayer. He would also instruct them that the manuscripts in his possession contained the teachings of his masters, and that the authorship should not be attributed to him.

*T*he tzaddik of Chernobel had a chassid, named Jeremiah. One day, while Jeremiah was praying, the tzaddik removed the tefillin from his head. "I had to do something to interrupt his prayer. He was approaching a state of devotion so intense that he was in danger of expiring."

This is a very sobering thought, and should help us realize just how far away we are from proper *kavannah* (concentration) in our prayers. It also sheds light on another form of *mesiras nefesh*.

Mesiras Nefesh of Prayer

arlier we referred to Rabbi Uri of Strelisk, whose devotion in prayer was so intense that he was in danger of his soul departing. There is yet another type of *mesiras nefesh* in prayer.

*M*y great-grandfather, the Rebbe of Hornostipol, was asked by a chassid, "Why is it that my prayers are unanswered? Were we not assured that G-d would grant the wishes of those who do His will? Why is it that the prayers of a tzaddik are more effective than the prayers of an average person?"

The Rebbe replied, "A person's sincere wish is never denied, but that wish must be the person's foremost desire, and very few people pray for what is truly their foremost desire.

"Take, for example, the person who prays for success and wealth. He may indeed be impoverished and may very profoundly desire to become wealthy. Yet, if he were drowning and could not catch his breath, he would, of course, not think of acquiring wealth. At that point, his most fervent and only desire would be to breathe and remain alive, hence wealth is not really his first priority.

"The Talmud states that if a person forgoes his own needs to pray for the needs of another, that prayer is warmly received.

"The devotion of a tzaddik to his followers is so great," the Rebbe continued, "that their well-being becomes his first priority. The love of the tzaddik for his fellow Jew surpasses the love and devotion of a father for his favorite child. When a tzaddik prays for someone's health and success, his desire for that person's happiness is so intense, that even if the tzaddik were drowning at that point, his prayer would not be for his own survival, nor his wish to be able to breathe and remain alive, but rather that the other person's needs be fulfilled. This self-negation and self-sacrifice which the tzaddik achieves out of love for his fellow man is the reason why his prayers are answered."

The Rebbe knew of what he spoke.

It is told that as a child, orphaned at a tender age, he was reared by his grandfather, the Rebbe of Cherkassy. Once one of the Rebbe's adherents came to Cherkassy to beg the Rebbe to pray for his salvation. He had not earned enough to meet the payments on the inn and dwelling which he was renting from the feudal lord, and the latter had threatened him with expulsion and imprisonment if his arrears were not promptly resolved. He could see no source of help, and asked the Rebbe to pray for Divine mercy, so that he and his family would not languish in prison.

To his horror he found that the Rebbe was out of the city, and when he approached the Rebbetzin with his bitter plight, she suggested, "Go to the house of study and talk to my grandson. He may be able to help you."

"But your grandson is only a child of 10," the man said. "I need the Rebbe. Our very lives are in jeopardy."

Again the Rebbetzin said, "The Rebbe is not available now. Go talk with my grandson."

The man went to the house of study, where the 10-year-old child was engrossed in Talmud studies, and against his better judgment, unburdened himself to the young boy. The young boy listened sympathetically to the man's tearful tale of woe, sighed deeply, and said, "If only my grandfather were here, I am certain that he could help you. But there is nothing I can do for you."

In desperation, the man cried out, "Look, your grandmother sent me to you. Now, if you truly cannot help me, then I hold no grudge against you. But if you have the capacity to help me and refrain from doing so, then I shall never forgive you for what will befall my family. Not only will I not forgive you in this world, but I will not forgive you in the eternal world as well."

The young boy was shaken. He slowly closed the volume of the Talmud and said, "Well, let us go first to the mikveh."

The man accompanied the young boy to the mikveh and stood by as the latter immersed himself beneath the surface of the water. After a few moments, the man became concerned that the child was not coming out of the water, and as the moments passed, far beyond what seemed to be the human endurance for surviving without air, the man became panic stricken. He tried to go down to the mikveh to extricate the child, but his limbs seemed to be paralyzed. He soon forgot about his troubles, about his being in arrears, and about his imminent eviction or imprisonment. He was totally occupied with the child whose head remained immersed beneath the water. "Dear G-d," he prayed silently and fervently, "just let me see that young child emerge from the mikveh alive."

After what seemed to be not one but many eternities, the young boy emerged from the water. "Go home," he said. "You have nothing to worry about."

Several weeks later, the chassid returned to the Rebbe of Cherkassy and told him that upon his return home, the feudal lord had sent for him and apologized to him for having been so harsh with him. That previous night, the feudal lord related, he developed a choking sensation and was unable to breathe. In his panic he began to reflect that perhaps he was being punished by G-d for being so ruthless with his tenants. He then resolved the henceforth he would be more lenient with them, and soon thereafter his breathing returned to normal. "So," he said, "I will not only forgive you your arrears but I will also arrange more liberal terms for your future payments."

The Rebbe of Cherkassy shook his head sadly, "This is too tender an age for him to place his life in jeopardy."

The pattern that was initiated at age 10 persisted for the next 53 years. The wants and needs of others took priority, always.

Tzaddikim who had given themselves over totally to *klal Yisrael,* and had *mesiras nefesh* for their people, were forever on the alert to plead Israel's cause before G-d. One such incident occurred with the *Maggid* of Koznitz.

A woman complained to the Maggid that her husband had rejected her, saying that she was no longer attractive and he had lost his affection for her. The Maggid was deeply moved by this woman's plight and said, "I will certainly try and talk with your husband, but unfortunately, there are some people who will not listen to reason. If your husband has fallen under the domination of his yetzer hara I may not be able to move him."

"But that is not fair," the woman cried. "When he married me I was young and beautiful. Now that I have grown old and have lost the beauty of my youth, he abandons me! There is no justice in this."

The Maggid's eyes welled up, and tears began pouring out profusely. He lifted his face toward heaven and said, "Master of the universe, we, Your people, were once young and beautiful. We left Egypt and followed You into a barren desert, not knowing from where our food and water were to come, but we had faith in You. And now that we have lost the beauty of our youth, is it fair that You allow us to be persecuted among the nations? Is it just that You abandon us? Master of the universe, I may not be able to convince this woman's husband to take her back, but You are infinite in compassion and kindness, and Your justice is without fault. Surely You will take us back."

While verbal prayer is important, it is not the highest degree of prayer.

A student in the yeshivah of Radin developed epilepsy, and in those days there were no effective medications to prevent convulsions. The student pleaded with the Chafetz Chaim, "Help me, Rabbi, for otherwise I am doomed."

The Chafetz Chaim tried to calm the young man, and said to him, "Listen carefully to me, my son. You must promise that you will never reveal this to a living soul. You should travel to this particular village, and ask the local rabbi for his blessing. With G-d's help, you will be healed."

The student did as he was told, and received the blessing of the village rabbi. The latter was perplexed why he had come for a blessing to him, since he was not in anyway more pious than the average rabbi.

The student eventually became seizure-free, married, and had a family. He shared his history with his wife.

Some years later, the wife's brother developed epilepsy, and she asked her husband for the secret of his recovery. Having promised the Chafetz Chaim never to reveal it, the husband was most reluctant, but after unrelenting pressure, he told her the whole story.

Soon afterwards he began having seizures again. He traveled to the Chafetz Chaim, who was then in his 90s, and confessed that he had breached his promise, and would he have mercy on him and help him regain his health.

The Chafetz Chaim said, "Let me tell you the truth. When you came to me 30 years ago, I indeed prayed for you, but I also fasted 40 consecutive days, fervently praying for your recovery. Thank G-d, my prayers were accepted. At my present age, I am too frail and I can no longer undertake so strenuous a course. I see no way that I can help you."

What we see in this story is the effectiveness of prayer when it is sincere. The Chafetz Chaim's desire to help the student was so genuine that he willingly went 40 days without food or drink. It is of further interest that the Chafetz Chaim, in his profound humility, tried to divert attention from himself as the agent of procuring Divine healing, and made it appear as though the blessing of the village rabbi effected the cure.

In our generation we had a *tzaddik* who taught us something about prayer. When the Rabbi of Brisk, Rabbi Yitzchak Zev Soloveitchik, was asked to pray for a sick person, he would first make a donation to *tzedakah*, and then pray. He would inquire about the circumstances of the sick person. Does the patient have adequate medical help? Is there a need for additional medical services that the patient cannot afford? He would repeatedly inquire about the patient's progress. If there was anything that could be done to improve the patient's chances of recovery, Rabbi Soloveitchik would see to it that this was done.

Rabbi Soloveitchik cited the *Midrash,* which comments on the Biblical account of Pharaoh's daughter finding the infant Moses adrift in the Nile. The *Midrash* states that she reached for the box, and though it was out of reach the length of her arm miraculously extended and she retrieved it.

"Why did she even try for something that was beyond her reach?" the rabbi asked. "It is because we must always try, even when it appears futile. Nothing is impossible for G-d, but He wants us to make the initial effort.

"G-d heals the sick, but we must make every effort to do whatever we can for the patient. Praying for him is important, but it is not enough. A genuine interest in the patient's welfare, which includes looking at and providing for his needs, is what merits G-d's merciful healing."

Praying for others means that we have consideration for them, and the reason that sincere prayer qualifies as *mesiras nefesh* is because we must give up something if we genuinely feel for others.

The Talmud tells us that one of the noble traits of Rabbi Zeira was that "he never rejoiced in another person's misfortune" (*Megillah* 28a). But why would this be considered a quality of greatness? Only a degenerate person would gloat over someone else's troubles. One of the commentaries therefore explains that Rabbi Zeira could never fully rejoice in his own *simchos.* He so identified and empathized with those who were in distress that the suffering of others distracted from his well-deserved personal joy.

Genuinely caring for others and praying for them may be at the cost of one's own comfort, and this is why it is *mesiras nefesh.*]

An outstanding example of *mesiras nefesh* involving prayer is found in the Maharal's comment on the verse in *Genesis* (46:29) which describes the reunion of Jacob and Joseph after 22 years of separation, with Jacob's belief that his beloved son was dead. The Torah states that Joseph wept as they embraced. Rashi states that Jacob did not weep, because he was reciting the *Shema.*

The Maharal asks, "Isn't this a rather unusual time to recite the *Shema*, just at the moment of reunion after so long and painful an absence?" He goes on to explain that precisely because Jacob experienced so intense a feeling of love, and so profound an emotional experience, perhaps the like of which he had never felt before, that he reasoned, "An intense emotion of this magnitude should not be permitted to be spent on anything other than my relationship with G-d," and he therefore recited the *Shema*, in order to invest it with the highest degree of passion he had ever experienced. He could now say the *ve'ahavta*, declaring his love for G-d in a manner heretofore unaccessible to him. This is a *living mesiras nefesh* at its finest.

Honor Your Father And Mother

There are few mitzvos in the Torah that receive the emphasis and respect that the Talmud gives to the mitzvah of honoring one's parents. The Talmud states, "There are three partners in a person: G-d, and one's father and mother. When a person respects his father and mother, G-d says, 'I consider it as though I lived with them and they were honoring Me.' On the other hand, if a person is disrespectful to his parents, G-d says, 'It is good that I did not dwell among them, for otherwise they would have caused Me great distress' (*Kiddushin* 30b, 31a). The Talmud considers giving proper respect to one's parents to be one of the most difficult mitzvos to observe, and one whose reward is unusually great (*Jerusalem Talmud, Peah* 1:1).

The *Seder Hadoros* (Page 66) relates the following story.

R abbi Yehoshua ben Elam was told in a dream, "Re-joice, because you and the diminutive butcher will share a place in Gan Eden (Paradise) for your portion and his are equal." When Rabbi Yehoshua awoke he said, "Woe is to me. From the day I was born I always stood in reverence of G-d, and was always devoted to the study of Torah. I never walked without tzitzis and tefillin, and I have 80 scholarly students. And now I am told that all of my good deeds and all of my Torah study is equal to those of an ordinary butcher."

Rabbi Yehoshua wandered from village to village and town to town, looking for this diminutive butcher. He finally came to one town where there was a butcher who was indeed of small stature, and when he asked to have him brought before him, the townsfolk said, "Why would you want to meet someone who is such a simple, uneducated person?" When he nevertheless persisted, several of the townspeople went to the butcher and told him that Rabbi Yehoshua wished to talk to him. "That is impossible," the butcher said, "because so great a personage would have nothing to do with someone like me. You are only mocking me." Rabbi Yehoshua then went to the butcher's home, and the latter bowed before him and said, "You are the crown of our people. Why would you come to see someone as insignificant as me?"

Rabbi Yehoshua said, "Please tell me, what is it that you do?" The butcher replied, "I am a butcher, and I try to do my work honestly. I have an elderly father and mother who are unable to get about, and everyday I bathe them, dress them, feed them, and lead them to wherever they wish to go."

Rabbi Joshua embraced the butcher and kissed him on his forehead saying, "How fortunate are you, and how for-

tunate am I that I merited to share a place in Gan Eden with you."

The mitzvah of honoring one's parents was always very special in the Jewish home. Unfortunately, circumstances in modern times sometimes make it difficult to observe this mitzvah properly. In many families, both husband and wife may have to work in order to support the family properly, and with both being away from the house most of the day, an elderly parent who requires care might not be able to be left at home alone. In some instances, the children can hire a person to look after the elderly parent while they are away at work, but sometimes this is not possible. It is truly unfortunate that parents may be placed in homes for the elderly, and although this may be inevitable when they reach a stage of aging where care at home is not feasible, it often happens that they are placed in residential settings at a time when they still could function or be cared for at home.

There is no question that providing care at home is difficult and may place considerable stress on the other members of the household. However, in those situations where care at home is feasible, every effort should be made to maintain the elderly parent within the home setting, although this may require *mesiras nefesh.*

We may not be aware of how susceptible we are to prevailing attitudes. During the 1960s, there was a major upheaval in social norms, and young people developed the attitude that their seniors were either ignorant or obsolete, or both. There was a major deterioration in respect for authority across the board, and the attitude toward parental authority suffered a great deal. People who were committed to observance of Torah perhaps withstood this onslaught a bit better, but even here the derogatory attitude toward one's elders may have had some effect. Traditionally, children addressed their parents with the greatest reverence, and one would not think of sitting in the place usually occupied by one's father or mother. It is of utmost importance that we strengthen our resolve to observe this precious mitzvah in the finest way, even though it may impinge upon our convenience and comfort.

On several occasions I have pointed out that *mesiras nefesh* may appear to call for sacrifice, but that ultimately it is to our own benefit.

I recall my father reprimanding a man for having placed his elderly mother in a home for the aged. This man was very wealthy, and could easily have provided household help and kept his mother in her familiar surroundings. My father said to him, "You should be aware that your children are observing what you are doing. They are very likely to emulate you, and you may well expect that when you reach old age, they will have you placed in a residential facility as well." Thus, when we demonstrate to our children how we revere our parents and care for them, we are setting an example that may serve us well.

Respecting one's parents also indicates one's attitude toward life as a whole. People who are derelict in respect for their parents may say, "I owe them nothing. I did not ask to be born. They brought me into this world, therefore they should provide for my comfort. Given all the difficulties in life, had I had a choice, I would have preferred not to have been born." Such an attitude conveys a philosophy of life that existence is not an unqualified good.

The Torah attitude is otherwise. A Torah-observant person considers his existence, an opportunity to serve G-d, to be a privilege. Even though the vicissitudes of life may be distressing, he nevertheless considers it to be a blessing to be able to elevate his *neshamah* by proper observance of Torah and mitzvos. He is grateful to his parents for having brought him into existence.

As with other behaviors, we can learn much from the lives of our great *tzaddikim*.

*R*abbi Zundel was once found to be smoothing out the ground in front of the shul. He explained to the on-lookers, "During the rains, the ground became muddy and very uneven, and remained very rough as it hardened. My mother walks this path when she comes to shul, and I wanted to be sure that she has a smooth path from her home to the shul."

*O*ne time a man asked Rabbi Chaim Soloveitchik of Brisk whether he is required to travel to visit his ailing father, since the halachah exempts a person from going into expense for this mitzvah. Rabbi Chaim responded, "You are correct. You do not have to go to the expense of buying a ticket to travel to your father. You can get there by walking."

*T*he chassidic master, the Yehudi of P'shischa, was once lecturing on a very complicated portion of the Talmud. The subject under discussion seemed to be incredibly difficult, and conflicts within the text could not be resolved. The Yehudi then gave his students a break, and said that he would resume discussion of this difficult issue when they reassembled.

One student, who was very hungry, ran home to grab a bite, and as he was about to leave, his mother asked him to bring down some wood from the loft. The young man replied, "Please forgive me, Mother, but I must hurry back to the lecture, because I do not wish to miss any of the discussion." The mother nodded and said, "Go right ahead, and learn well." As soon as the young man left the house he paused and reflected, "What is the purpose of my learning Torah if not to implement it in everyday life? What can I gain from a theoretical understanding of the Talmud if I do *not put its teachings to use?" He then turned around, went back home, and brought down the wood his mother had requested.*

The student hurried back to the house of study, and after he entered, the Yehudi greeted him, saying, "What wonderful mitzvah have you just done? When you entered, the Amora cited in this portion of the Talmud, Abaye, accompanied you, and in a moment he resolved the conflict which had stumped us."

The student then told the master about his deliberation and his ultimate decision to return home and fetch the wood for his mother. The Yehudi then said, "Of course! You see Abaye was orphaned of both parents at a very young age, and never had the opportunity to fulfill this mitzvah. Hence, when you entered, the spirit of Abaye that accompanied you illuminated this difficult portion of the Talmud for me."

Problems in *halachah* may occur in the kitchen, and it is common practice for people to seek the ruling of a Torah authority when such problems arise. The mitzvah of honoring one's parents is also carefully regulated by *halachah,* and we should not rely on our own unaided sense of judgment to make decisions in this most important area. Implementing this mitzvah may indeed require *mesiras nefesh.*

Love Your Neighbor

O ne of the outstanding mitzvos is *ahavas Yisrael*, love for another person. The Baal Shem Tov said that inasmuch as G-d is abstract and intangible, it may be difficult to develop love for Him. The royal road of love to G-d, said the Baal Shem Tov, is *ahavas Yisrael*. Many *tzaddikim* excelled in *ahavas Yisrael*. Perhaps most prominent in Chassidic folklore is Rabbi Levi Yitzchak of Berditchev, who was constantly interceding with G-d on behalf of His people.

F or example, Rabbi Levi Yitzchak once encountered a man who was eating on Tishah b'Av.

"My child," he said, "you must have forgotten that today is Tishah b'Av."

"No, I know it is Tishah b'Av," the man replied.

"Ah, then you have been instructed by your doctor that you may not fast because of poor health."

"I am perfectly healthy," the man said.

Rabbi Levi Yitzchak raised his eyes toward heaven. "Master of the universe," he said. "I have given this man two opportunities to exonerate himself for eating on Tishah b'Av, but he is so dedicated to truth that he rejected my offer, even at the risk of incriminating himself.

"You are a G-d of truth, and here is a man who is so devoted to truth. Isn't he a true tzaddik?"

It takes little effort to have love for a *tzaddik*. The trick is to be able to love those who appear to be undeserving of love. One of the chassidic masters said, "I wish I could have the love for the greatest *tzaddik* that G-d has for the worst *rasha*." And again, "It does not bother me if I am derelict in failing to despise someone who deserves to be despised, but I am terribly frightened of being derelict in failing to love someone who deserves to be loved."

The Torah tells us "Love your neighbor as yourself," and some people have observed this mitzvah with *mesiras nefesh*. In this case the *mesiras nefesh* is contained in the words "as yourself." The attitude towards another person should be no different than toward oneself.

For example, the *Jerusalem Talmud* states that a person should not seek revenge against someone who had harmed or offended him, anymore than if one had injured his left hand, he would hit it with his right hand as punishment for having caused him pain. If one truly feels identified with others "as yourself," one would not take revenge against another just as one would not take revenge against oneself. But to feel this way requires *mesiras nefesh*, a turning over of oneself to others.

Not only is it forbidden to take revenge, but it is also forbidden to complain to G-d about having been wronged by another person in a way that one is asking G-d to punish that person. The Matriarch Sarah was humiliated by Hagar, whom she had given to Abraham as a concubine. The Talmud states that because Sarah complained to G-d and asked that Hagar be punished, she herself was punished first in that she died prematurely. According to *Maharsha* (*Bava Kamma* 93a) Sarah was destined to reach the age of Abraham, 175, but because she had asked G-d to punish Hagar, she forfeited 48 years of her life. Inasmuch as prayer can be effective in thought as well as verbally, we must be careful to avoid even wishing harm to someone who has offended us. This is heavy duty, and we can see why it requires *mesiras nefesh*.

The *neshamah* is part of G-d Himself, and G-d is absolute unity. Therefore, all *neshamos* are essentially one. We are separate and distinct beings by virtue of our physical bodies. To the extent that we emphasize our physical component, the body, to that extent we are separate and distinct from one another. To the extent that we minimize the importance of the body relative to the soul, and give the *neshamah* primacy, to that extent we are one, and can feel for another the way we feel for ourselves. People who excel in *ahavas Yisrael* had this kind of *mesiras nefesh*, having achieved a state of spirituality where the body became subordinate to the *neshamah,* and they turned over their soul (lit. *mesiras nefesh*) to be one with the souls of others.

The Patriarch Abraham referred to himself as being "only dust and ash" (*Genesis* 18:27). Ibn Ezra states that this refers to the fact that G-d said to Adam, "For you are dust and to dust you will return" (*Genesis* 3:19). Abraham's comment was in the context of his pleading to G-d to spare the sinful city of Sodom. The Patriarch's intense intervention on behalf of the corrupt city was due to the fact that he had achieved so great an effacement of the body that he was capable of extraordinary empathy, even to the degree of pleading for mercy for the most sinful. To Abraham, his physical body was nothing but a handful of dust, and did not stand in the way of the expression of the needs of his *neshamah*.

Undoubtedly, *tzaddikim* were always searching for means of improving their level of performance of mitzvos.

The Maggid of Chernobel was active in pidyon she-vuyim, obtaining the release of Jews who had been imprisoned by their poritzim, the feudal lords who incarcerated their vassals at their slightest whim. One time the Maggid was himself incarcerated on the false accusation that he was a sympathizer of the revolution.

The Maggid was visited in prison by one of the tzaddikim who said, "Why did G-d instruct the Patriarch Abraham to leave his homeland? It is because Abraham practiced the mitzvah of hachnassas orchim, hospitality to travelers. G-d therefore said, 'What you are doing is indeed commendable, but you cannot fully understand the needs of the traveler unless you have been one yourself. Therefore, leave your homeland and become a wanderer. You will then have greater appreciation for what you can do to be helpful to a wayfarer.'

"So it is with you," the tzaddik said to the Maggid. "You have indeed performed the mitzvah of pidyon shevuyim. But you could never fully appreciate the agony of what it means to be in a dungeon. Now that you are personally experiencing it, you will increase your dedication to this great mitzvah."

The Maggid was overjoyed. He now understood that his suffering in prison was not in vain, and that it would help him in further developing his spirituality by better performance of the mitzvah. Feeling the anguish of being imprisoned would enhance his mesiras nefesh, his identifying with his imprisoned brethren.

When the Maggid subsequently learned that a Jew was put into the dungeon by his poritz for being in arrears on his rent, and was being held hostage until the rent was paid, he sent his chassidim to raise the ransom money. He then offered himself as hostage so that the imprisoned Jew could be home with his family on Shabbos.

There are hundreds of accounts of how people practice *chessed* (kindness) to others. Even extraordinary self-effacement was not felt to be a sacrifice. After all, they were not really doing anything for strangers. Rather, having totally identified themselves with others, they felt that they were doing for themselves. It can hardly be considered a sacrifice if one does something for oneself.

The tzaddik of Stitchin would welcome wayfarers into his home and provide them with a place to sleep, even if they were dressed in tattered clothes and covered with the dust of the road. When it was pointed out to him that they might be carrying insects that would infest his bedclothes, the tzaddik said, "The Talmud states that the dead body actually feels the pain of being worm eaten. At that time I will not be able to do anything to the insects that will be irritating me. Is it not better that I take the risk of being bitten by insects in this world, where I can at least brush the insects away, and hope that by merit of the mitzvah of hachnassas orchim, I will be spared the misery after death?"

A similar story is told of Rabbi Liebr of Berditchev.

Rabbi Leibr was preparing a bed for a wayfarer. The latter protested and said, " It is not proper for a personage like you to be preparing a bed for me." Rabbi Liebr re-

sponded, "You are mistaken. I am not preparing a bed only for you in this world. I am preparing a comfortable bed for myself in the eternal world."

How far can *mesiras nefesh* go in concern for another person?

A chassid of Rabbi Schneur Zalman once complained that he had five daughters, several of whom were of marriageable age, but has been unable to find a match for them. He felt that since he was an insignificant person, a lowly cheder teacher, no one wished to have him in their family. Rabbi Schneur Zalman responded, "I will take one of your daughters for one of my sons, and then everybody will wish to associate with you." Rabbi Schneur Zalman indeed did so, taking the teacher's daughter for his son Rabbi Dov Ber, who was to be his successor. Incidentally, this extraordinary act of chessed resulted in illustrious descendants who became the leaders of Lubavitch chassidim during the past two centuries. Inasmuch as I trace my lineage to Rabbi Dov Ber, this obscure cheder teacher is one of my ancestors.

For our great *tzaddikim* to give up precious time from their study of Torah was indeed an act of *mesiras nefesh*. The noted sage of the past generation, Rabbi Isser Zalman Meltzer, was extremely diligent not to allow even one moment to be idle of Torah study. Yet, if he was invited to a wedding, and he felt that his presence at the wedding would enhance the joy of the wedding party, he would give up his Torah study for the act of chessed, to participate in the wedding festivities.

Every thinking person searches for meaning in life, and it should be obvious that there can be meaning for an individual only if there is meaning to the world as a whole. People who do not believe in Creation and who assume that the universe is the result of accidental happenings in primeval matter and energy (which came from where?) cannot achieve a true sense of meaning. It is absurd to speak of purpose of life in a world that is purposeless.

The Scripture says that the world was created with and for *chessed* (*Psalms* 89:3). With *chessed* as the purpose for the very existence of the world, pursuit of *chessed* can become the purpose of an individual's life.

It was not only great *tzaddikim* who were capable of acts of *chessed*. Many ordinary people excelled in *chessed* as well.

I recall a man in the community in which I grew up. Mike Ehrlich was hardly a scholar. He would listen to a discussion of the Mishnah, but I can assure you that he did not understand a single word of what was said.

Mike took ill and was hospitalized, suffering much pain. One of the shul members visited him and found him to be in severe agony, but in surprisingly good spirits. Mike said to him, "I have reached an agreement with G-d, that he accept my suffering in exchange for anything that might be destined to happen to the Rabbi's family. I feel happy that I am able to spare the Rabbi's family from any misery."

Yes, Mike was able to achieve *mesiras nefesh*.

The Torah states that we are required to attach ourselves to G-d. But how can a mere mortal attach himself to the Infinite? By emulating G-d's traits, says the Talmud. "Just as G-d is merciful, so must you be merciful."

Anytime one does an act of *chessed*, one is uniting himself with G-d, and that constitutes *mesiras nefesh*.

Suffering With Love

ne of the most difficult concepts in Judaism is *yesurim b'ahavah* (suffering with love). This presents itself in two aspects: *kabbalas yesurim b'ahavah,* accepting suffering with love, and *es asher ye'ehav Hashem yochiach,* G-d may impose suffering on those whom He loves (*Proverbs* 3:12). The explanation usually given for the latter is that a person may be put through suffering in this world, which is only a temporary existence, in order to increase his reward in Heaven, which is an eternal existence. I must admit that this was very difficult to understand. If G-d wishes to give someone greater reward in Heaven, why is it necessary for one to experience suffering while alive?

Rabbi Chaim of Chernovitz, in his work *Siduro Shel Shabbos* sheds some light on this problem in his discussion of a difficult *Midrash*. G-d showed Moses the entire future of Israel, with each generation and its leaders. He showed him the great Talmudic sage, Rabbi Akiva, who was the key to the transmittal of the entire Talmud (*Yevamos* 62b). Moses was overjoyed with Rabbi Akiva's enormous erudition and teaching, but when he saw that Rabbi Akiva would be tortured and would die a martyr's death, he protested, "Is this the reward for devoting one's life to Torah study?" G-d responded, "Be silent! This is the thought that has been before Me" (*Menachos* 29b). How are we to understand this *Midrash?*

The Talmud and homiletic works state that G-d conducts the world according to a rigid system of justice, as the Scripture states, "The king establishes the land by law" (*Proverbs* 29:4). Every action a person does is recorded, and both reward and punishment are meted out justly. One may not assume that G-d will overlook the slightest act (*Bava Kamma* 50a). There is forgiveness for a sin where a person has merited forgiveness by proper, sincere *teshuvah,* but there is no gratis "overlooking" anything.

The heavenly system of law operates quite similarly to an earthly judicial system. There is a prosecutor, representing Satan, and a defender, representing the angel Michael. Judgments are delivered on the basis of consideration of the evidence and deliberation. Just as an earthly judge has some latitude within the law, so does G-d have latitude, but G-d never violates His laws.

There is a principle that G-d rewards good thoughts as if they were good deeds. However, since a person's thoughts are known only to G-d Himself and not to angels, the thoughts cannot be presented before the heavenly tribunal as evidence of one's virtue.

When Rabbi Akiva was being tortured prior to his execution, his disciples said, "Master, is this how far it must go?" Rabbi

Akiva responded, "My entire life I have been aspiring to offer my life to G-d, and now that I have the opportunity I have prayed for, shall I decline it?" We see then that Rabbi Akiva had repeatedly pledged himself to accept martyrdom to sanctify G-d's Name, and for this he was to receive boundless reward in heaven. However, precisely because the reward was so great, the adversary might challenge its legitimacy, and claim that there was no proof that Rabbi Akiva was indeed so sincerely dedicated that he would have actually offered his life. Intentions are one thing, and enacting them is another. Rabbi Akiva might then have been deprived of the rich reward he deserved. G-d therefore brought him to the reality of martyrdom, which validated the truth of his intentions, following which he would then reap the reward for his years of dedication.

This, then, may be how *yesurim shel ahavah* operate. It is a means whereby a person may secure the reward which is justly his, but which requires adequate proof before the heavenly tribunal.

One may deduce from this that by having a sincere dedication for *mesiras nefesh*, whether that of martyrdom or a *living mesiras nefesh*, one is rendering oneself vulnerable to be tested. This is indeed so, but what is the option? If we are not sincere in our beliefs and willing to put them to the test, of what value are they?

We should also realize that advancing oneself spiritually may subject one to more stringent tests. The Talmud states that the Patriarch, Abraham, was put to 10 tests and that he withstood them all, which proved his love for G-d (*Ethics of the Fathers* 5:3). We might ask: How does this prove his love for G-d? Perhaps he acted out of fear rather than love.

There is an axiom that G-d will not test a person with a challenge that is beyond one's capacity. People of lesser strength will not be put to a test that requires more endurance than they possess. By the same token, as one advances in spiritual development and one's character strength increases, one becomes more vulnerable to more demanding challenges.

After experiencing the first few tests, the Patriarch Abraham accurately sized up the situation. As he was growing in spirituality, as he was drawing himself closer to G-d, his trials were becoming more severe. Someone other than Abraham might have decided to cut his losses and arrest his spiritual growth. What point is there in becoming more spiritual if this will result in being confronted with ever harsher challenges? But Abraham's love for G-d was so great that he willingly accepted the consequences that would accrue from his coming closer to G-d. He wished to strengthen his relationship with G-d at all costs, in full knowledge of what demands this may make of him. And indeed, Abraham arrived at so great a level of devotion to G-d that he was put to the ultimate test of whether he would sacrifice his only child to G-d if required to do so. And as we know, Abraham triumphed over this challenge as well. This is what proved Abraham's love for G-d.

This, too, is a *living mesiras nefesh*: accepting, as Abraham did, the possibility of experiencing suffering, being put to ever increasing trials and tests of one's faith as one advances in spiritual growth, and doing so willingly out of the conviction that the only meaningful life is one that is dedicated to the fulfillment of the Divine will.

Torah Study

owhere is the concept of *living mesiras nefesh* spelled out more clearly then in regard to the study of Torah, about which the Talmud states, "Torah cannot have any existence unless one is willing to give his life for it" (*Shabbos* 83b). Obviously, the Talmud is not referring to martyrdom, but rather to giving Torah study such priority that everything else becomes secondary.

There are numerous references to Torah being identical with life itself, as we say in our evening prayers, "for the words of Torah are our very life." The full impact of this concept can be gathered from the *halachah* that specifies that if a student kills someone accidentally and must therefore take up residence in one of the designated cities of refuge, his teacher must accompany him. This is based on the verse in the Torah that "he (the perpetrator) shall flee to one of the cities of refuge and *shall live* (*Deuteronomy* 4:42), which the Talmud interprets as "you must provide him with the means to live," and that means someone who will teach him Torah.

Think of it! This young man must go into exile for an indefinite period because he accidentally killed someone, and now his teacher must uproot himself and take up what may well be permanent residence in a distant city, because otherwise the student would be deprived of Torah, and it is unthinkable to inflict such deprivation on this person. Just as it would not be conscionable to punish this inadvertent act by depriving the student of food and water, the bare essentials of life, so it is unconscionable to deprive him of Torah, for that, too, is an essential of life.

There are innumerable accounts of the overwhelming importance of Torah study.

*R*abbi Ephraim Margolis was a Torah scholar who was also a wealthy merchant. He gave instructions that he was not to be disturbed while studying Torah. One time his wife told him that several important business people wished to see him regarding a venture that would result in a huge profit. Rabbi Margolis replied, "Torah knowledge cannot be achieved unless one is willing to die for it. Had I died, these people could not transact with me. For now, let them consider it as though I had died." When he later discovered the magnitude of the financial loss he had sustained by rejecting this opportunity, he cheerfully said, "Thank G–d, I was able to acquire a page of Talmud for only several thousand gulden."

The sages state, "This is the way of Torah: Eat bread with salt, drink water by the measure, and sleep on the earth" (*Ethics of the Fathers* 6:4), by which is meant that unless one is willing to forgo many comforts and pleasures in life, one cannot aspire to acquisition of Torah. The point is not that one must live in deprivation, but that Torah must be given so high a priority that if the only way to achieve it would require radical deprivation, one must be willing to accept this.

The *Midrash* states that the Torah was given in the Sinai desert to teach us that only if one is ready to live a barren life, devoid of all comforts, can one acquire Torah. It was given on Sinai, the lowest of all the hills in the area, to teach us that only if one effaces himself and divests himself of all ego needs, can one acquire Torah.

Throughout the ages, young men left the comforts of home to fulfill the Talmudic instruction "Exile yourself to a place of Torah" (*Ethics of the Fathers* 4:14). They did so even if there were adequate Torah study resources at home. Why? Because the comforts and conveniences of home might detract from diligence in Torah study. Many of our great Torah scholars did not even have the benefit of a yeshivah dormitory or kitchen. They slept on benches and ate "days," i.e., they were assigned days at the homes of local residents where they could have a meal. It was this *living mesiras nefesh* that gave us the Torah giants that grace our proud heritage.

For these giants of Torah, nothing took precedence to their Torah study.

The Gaon of Vilna was once visited by his sister, whom he had not seen for several years. He arose, recited the blessing of Shehecheyanu, thanking G–d for the opportunity to see a loved one, and then said, "My dear sister, in the next world we will have abundant time to converse. In this world we must devote ourselves to Torah," and promptly returned to his studies.

There are many anecdotes of how Torah scholars utilized every single available moment for Torah study. Some used to immerse their feet in ice water when they became sleepy, to arouse them from their drowsiness so that sleep should not rob them of precious moments of Torah study. We are not referring here to ancients, but to our own contemporaries. I recall one Torah scholar who would apply cold compresses to his forehead to banish sleepiness.

It is worthwhile to study the sixth chapter of *Ethics of the Fathers,* which lists the uniqueness of Torah and the prerequisites for its acquisition. In *Mishnah* 6, 48 qualities are listed which are essential for acquisition of Torah. These are: study, attentive listening, articulate speech, intuitive understanding, discernment, awe, reverence, modesty, joy, purity, ministering to the sages, closeness with colleagues, sharp discussion with students, deliberation, knowledge of Scripture, knowledge of *Mishnah,* limited business activity, limited sexual activity, limited pleasure, limited sleep, limited conversation, limited joviality, slowness to anger, a good heart, faith in the sages, acceptance of suffering, knowing one's place, being happy with one's lot, making a protective fence around his personal matters, claiming no credit for oneself, being beloved, loving G–d, loving His creatures, loving righteous ways, loving justice, loving acceptance of reproof, avoiding seeking acclaim, not being arrogant with one's learning, not enjoying exercising halachic decision-making, sharing in one's fellow yoke, judging others favorably, setting others on the truthful course, setting others on a peaceful course, thinking deliberately in one's study, asking and answering, listening and contributing to the discussion, learning in order to teach, learning in order to practice, making one's teacher wiser, pondering over what one has learned, and repeating a saying in the name of one who said it.

Inasmuch as the Talmud considers these prerequisites, it follows that to the degree that one is lacking in these, one is lacking in Torah. Obviously, attainment of Torah calls for a *living mesiras nefesh.*

Yet, this *mesiras nefesh* need not constitute an intolerable burden. Torah is compared to diamonds, and in contrast to other merchandise which may be of great value only when present in great mass and constituting a heavy burden, Torah is never burdensome to those who appreciate its enormous value.

The requisites for Torah knowledge and Torah observance may appear formidable, but a bit of analysis will reveal why no other options are feasible.

We have noted that what we refer to as *mesiras nefesh* is in fact *mesiras haguf,* i.e., subordinating the body and one's physical drives to the will of the *neshamah.* We have also noted that the *guf* is essentially an animal entity, and although it may be a high-level animal with greater intellect than lower forms of life, pursuit of the aspirations of the *guf* renders a person's behavior essentially animalistic in nature. Not only should it be beneath one's pride to function at this level, but it may also result in depression and frustration if a person lives beneath his potential, and we have seen that the human being is capable of enormous spirituality.

One of the fundamental principles of *chassidus* and *mussar* is stated by Rabbi Schneur Zalman, and that is that *the mind or intellect has an inborn capacity to be master over the emotions* (*Tanya* Chapter 12). This is hardly a revolutionary concept, since every person at one time or another exercises restraint over a number of physical impulses. The works of *chassidus* and *mussar* simply extend this concept, and point out that spiritual growth requires placing more areas under the dominance of the *neshamah.* A bit of application of the intellect will show you why this is is what every intelligent human being should pursue. Physical desires are, without exception, ephemeral in nature, and many have the addictive quality of requiring greater and greater quantities to provide the sought-after gratification. This is why people who crave acclaim are always striving for more recognition and praise, and why those who crave riches continue to exert themselves in increasing their wealth even if they already have more money than they could use in six lifetimes, and why the gratification of lust is as futile as filling a bottomless pit. Alcohol and narcotics are not the only substances whose use may lead to serious and even fatal addiction. Many people are addicted to food or to nicotine, and these addictions stand right alongside those of cocaine and heroin.

Torah living requires pursuit of truth, and coming closer to G–d means incorporating truth into one's being. Every time we recite the *Shema* we allude to the words of the prophet, "G–d is truth" (*Jeremiah* 10:10), and if one seeks to identify with G–d, one must live a life of truth.

In contrast to physical gratifications, which are all transient in nature, truth is eternal. You have long since forgotten the taste of a delicacy you ate, and the money you enjoyed earning has been spent. However, the Torah you learned many years ago remains with you and is integrated in your behavior even if you have forgotten it, and this holds true for all proper performances of mitzvos.

You may recall the story of Avi, the recovered, ex-convict drug addict who found an envelope with 5,000 shekalim and returned it to its rightful owner. When I complimented him on this he said, "You know, Doctor, in the years that I used heroin, I would experience the 'high' of the drug for 20 minutes or so, and then not only did the euphoria disappear, but I felt depressed in the aftermath of its use. The incident with the money I found happened four months ago, and I still enjoy it now, every time I think of it." This is the nature of mitzvos. Since they are G–dly in origin, they partake of Divine eternity, and the good feelings of having done a mitzvah persists long after the pleasures of indulgence have disappeared.

Rabbi Schneur Zalman was right in stressing that in every person there is the capacity for the intellect to dominate the emotions. Just a bit of clear thought will convince a person that it is far better to have a spiritual pleasure which is eternal than a momentary pleasure of gratifying a physical drive. If we fail to subject the *guf* to the *neshamah*, it is only because we fail to exercise our intellect, and allow the animal component of our person to dominate. We should be too proud to do something which is so far beneath our dignity.

The *mesiras nefesh* of students for Torah was surpassed only by that of their teachers, who dedicated their lives to their students. The Talmud says, "If one teaches another person's child Torah, it is as though he had fathered him" (*Sanhedrin* 19b), and they indeed cared for their students as if they were their own children.

*O*ne scholar related that in his youth he arrived in Radin at night, and lay down to sleep on a bench in the study hall. He awoke in the morning to find himself covered with a blanket, and at his bedside stood the great sage, the Chafetz Chaim, with a basin and water and a towel. After the young man washed his hands, the Chafetz Chaim gave him some warm milk, assuming that the lad had not eaten during his journey to the yeshivah. This great sage, who never allowed a single moment to go to waste, had patiently stood at the bedside of this new student, waiting for him to awaken so that he could revitalize him.

*T*he Chafetz Chaim once came to the yeshivah of Lomza on a winter night, and walked through the deep snow that had blanketed the city. As he approached the yeshivah, he saw that the walk had been cleared to allow the students unimpeded access. He shook the snow from his shoes, and was grateful for this convenience, silently blessing the shamash for his consideration in shoveling the snow. The following morning, when he thanked the shammash, the latter told him, "I am not deserving of this praise. I must confess that I was hesitant to go out in the cold, and I did not shovel the walk."

It was later discovered that the Rosh Yeshivah, Rabbi Eliezer Shulevitz, had shoveled the walk himself in the *stealth of the night, so that the students would not have to walk through the deep snow.*

The secular world, too, has institutions of higher learning, and there may indeed be instructors who take a personal interest in some students, but it is highly doubtful that any college professor has demonstrated the devotion of Rabbi Nosson Tzvi Finkel, the dean of the yeshivah of Slabodka.

The great Torah luminary of our generation, Rabbi Aaron Kotler, recalled that when he was a youngster and afraid to walk home in the dark, Rabbi Finkel would accompany him until he was safely in his residence. It was not unusual for Rabbi Finkel to accompany a student to the clothing store to make sure that he was properly fitted.

If a student took sick, Rabbi Finkel made sure that he was cared for adequately, and that someone was always present to look after him. He would pray intensely for the student's recovery, and his prayers were often accompanied by profuse weeping as he prayed to G-d for the youngster's health. It was not unusual for him to fast for his students' recovery. His students related to him as to a father, and he exhibited mesiras nefesh for them as one might expect only of a biological parent.

Under communist rule in Soviet Russia, study of Torah was fraught with the harsh punishment of exile to a forced labor camp in Siberia or even death. Yet, both teachers of Torah and young students risked their lives, secretly teaching and learning Torah. This is not ancient history, and accounts of these brave people are related by contemporary witnesses. This living *mesiras nefesh* of the highest order gives literal interpretation to our reference to Torah as "being our life," and demonstrates to us that we are indeed capable, even in this day and age, of achieving the heights of spirituality.

Will the Real Self
Please Stand Up

Virtually all the Jewish ethical works cite *anivus* (humility) as the most desirable character trait. Absence of *anivus* results in *ga'avah* (vanity), which is considered to be so despicable a trait that although G–d states that he does not abandon even the worst sinner, vanity is so repulsive to Him that He cannot countenance the presence of a vain person (*Arachin* 15b). Humility is generally described as self-effacement, as setting aside one's ego drives, such as the desire for recognition and acclaim, or thinking of oneself as meritorious.

Here we encounter a semantic problem not unlike that mentioned in the Introduction, where we pointed out that what is generally referred to as *mesiras nefesh* is in reality *mesiras haguf.* If we think of humility as "self-effacement," then we are considering the "self" as being comprised of the ego drives. But this may not at all be true. The real "self" is the *neshamah,* which does not need to be effaced at all. Quite the contrary, in achieving *anivus* the *neshamah* is enhanced rather than effaced.

A woman who was paralyzed told of attending a wedding. "I danced along with everyone else. Of course, I could not move my feet, but I danced with my hands on the table. You see, when I became paralyzed I did not change. I am still the same person I was. It is just that this person is trapped in a body that is paralyzed."

This woman's perception is that the body is but *a container for the person,* and the person need not be affected by changes to the body. Similarly, when one sets aside bodily demands, one is not depriving the "person," since the true person may not desire things which the body craves. In the same manner we can think of the real "self" as being the *neshamah,* and the ego drives to which we are subject may actually be external to the "self."

If we follow this semantic observation to its logical conclusion, it turns out that if one is "selfish" in the sense that one wishes to satisfy the aspirations of the *neshamah,* the real "self," this is diametrically opposite to what we generally think of as being "selfish," because the latter refers to indulging the bodily desires or ego needs. It is thus possible to speak of a "selfishness" that is commendable.

We have spoken earlier of *mesiras nefesh* actually being preservation of life rather than a rejection or denial of life. This becomes even clearer as we gain a better understanding of what constitutes the true self.

The Baal Shem Tov explained that *anivus* can actually be selfish in both senses. He states that if a person is singled out for praise and honor, he may be "audited," as it were, by the heavenly tribunal as to whether he is indeed deserving of this. And, said the Baal Shem Tov, it is never good to be conspicuous and to have one's record reviewed. One of the reasons given for *tefillah betzibur*, praying together with a multitude, is that one's merits as an individual are not scrutinized when one is part of a group. (Anyone who has had his income tax return audited can easily understand the Baal Shem Tov's observation.) By achieving *anivus* and blending into the surroundings, one avoids calling attention to oneself.

Furthermore, it is impossible to gain a true self-awareness if one is vain. The Baal Shem Tov pointed out that if one wishes to see his reflection in the water, one must bend down low, because in an upright position one cannot see himself, and this is why the Scripture uses the metaphor "like the reflection of the face in the water" (*Proverbs* 27:19). Only when one humbles himself can he see the true image.

It is of interest that the Talmud relates an incident of a person discovering his true image in the water. Shimon the Tzaddik, the great High Priest, said, " I never partook of the offerings of a nazirite who had become tamei (impure) except for once. One time a young man came from the South with beautiful, flowing locks, and he was about to shave his head upon completion of his vow as a nazirite. I said to him, 'My son, what prompted you to cut your beautiful hair?' The lad responded, 'I was a shepherd watching my father's flocks, and I bent down and saw my image in the water, and was struck by the beauty of my hair. At that moment I felt a surge of vanity, and I realized that the yetzer hara was at work, trying to destroy me with vanity. I exclaimed, "No way will you lead me to destruction, making me take pride in earthly appearances which are so deceptive." And at that point I vowed, "I swear I will cut these locks in a ritual of Divine service," and I took upon myself the status of a nazirite.' " To this Shimon the Tzaddik responded by embracing and kissing the young man. "You are a true holy nazirite," he said (Nedarim 9b).

A deeper understanding of *anivus* will give us yet another interpretation for *mesiras nefesh*.

There are some who think that *anivus* requires a person to think of himself as being a total nothing, which would mean that one has to deny one's capacities and strengths. As a result of my emphasizing the importance of self-esteem in psychological well-being, I have been challenged as to how I can contradict the Torah requirement for *anivus*, as though the latter is incompatible with self-esteem.

Nothing could be further from the truth. Some of our great ethicists have clarified this issue. Let me quote just one of them. Rabbi Yehuda Leib Chasman says:

"It is obvious that an *anav* is not a person who does not know his essence and his personality strengths. This is a fool rather than an *anav*. An *anav* is one who fully recognizes his capacities, but knows that they are not of his own doing, but rather a gift and endowment by a benevolent G–d. The more one recognizes this, the truer is one's *anivus*" (*Ohr Yahel 3, Shemini*).

The need to feel significant and important appears to be universal. Some people are content with feeling significant and important to their family and friends. People who have feelings of inadequacy and unworthiness may take extreme measures to feel important, and I have addressed this in *Let Us Make Man* (*Traditional Press* 1987). In their desperation, they may strive for recognition and acclaim from others, but most often their needs are so vast that no amount of acclaim can satisfy them. They may therefore end up with a pursuit of acclaim which the Talmud describes as both futile and destructive. "Whoever pursues acclaim will find that it flees from him" (*Eiruvin* 13b), and "There are three things that exhaust a person's life: envy, lust, and pursuit of acclaim" (*Ethics of the Fathers* 5:28).

If a person were aware of his capacities and strengths and knew that there was much that he can achieve in the mission of his life, there would not be this desperate need for acclaim from others to provide him with a sense of worth.

The true *anav* is aware of his strengths. The Chafetz Chaim, whose *anivus* was unquestionable, took upon himself the role of being virtually the final authority on *halachah*. If he was not aware of his enormous Torah scholarship, how did he undertake such an awesome responsibility? I am certain that when he completed his epochal *Mishnah Berurah*, the Chafetz Chaim did not say, "Now the world will know who I am," but to the contrary, knowing his vast Talmudical knowledge, he sighed and said, "Given the great capacity with which G–d has blessed me, I have not even begun to fulfill my duties."

Rabbi Chasman was right. *Anivus* requires knowing the truth about oneself, and if one has great abilities, one should avoid vanity, which would be taking personal credit for these, and instead attribute them to G–d's benevolence.

The ascribing of one's strengths to G–d can be thought of as *mesiras nefesh*, for this, too, is contained in the words "turning over one's life to G–d," whereby one "turns over" the credit and ascribes one's personal strength to G–d, rather than assuming them to be all one's own doing.

For someone who has truly dedicated his life to the service of G–d, the words of our prayer "For the Torah is our life" are taken literally. Deviating from Torah is tantamount to forfeiting one's very life.

*T*he great sage, Rabbi Isser Zalman Meltzer, once asked a student on Chol HaMoed (the intermediate days of Pesach or Succos) to bring him a pen and paper. The student was perplexed, knowing that Rabbi Isser Zalman never wrote on Chol HaMoed, and thought that perhaps the tzaddik had forgotten what day it was. Noting his bewilderment, Rabbi Isser Zalman said, "I know it is Chol HaMoed, but I must write nevertheless. It is a matter of the *greatest urgency, an actual pikuach nefesh (matter of life and death)."*

After writing a few words and putting the slip of paper in his pocket, Rabbi Isser Zalman explained, "You see, on Chol HaMoed, many people come to visit me. There is always a vulnerability that in meeting many people I may detect some of their character defects. It is so easy to be blinded to the faults in oneself and yet see them clearly in others.

"It is important to bear in mind that the defects we see in others are but a reflection of our own faults, but we are very prone to forget this. By nature we are inclined to think better of ourselves and less of others. If this happens, we may fall into the trap of ga'avah (vanity). I therefore wrote a note for myself, and from time to time I take this slip of paper from my pocket, to remind me to focus on my own shortcomings rather than those of others."

The full impact of this anecdote cannot be appreciated unless one understands that Rabbi Isser Zalman would not deviate one iota from *halachah,* and would never have written on *Chol HaMoed* unless he truly considered it necessary to avert a grave danger. The possibility that by meeting so many people who were in fact far inferior to him might cause him to feel superior to them, and he would then have a touch of vanity, constituted a *pikuach nefesh* for him.

It is not easy to achieve such a level of spirituality, but we can better understand how such an attitude can enable a person to have a *living mesiras nefesh.*

Beyond Human Capacity

related the following story in *Generation to Generation* (CIS 1987) and it was received with mixed reviews. It is a story about the great chassidic master, Rebbe Nachum of Chernobel, who was a disciple of the Baal Shem Tov and of the *Maggid* of Mezeritch, and who was the first of the Twerski family. To say that Rabbi Nachum was a devoted father is a gross understatement. Many fathers are loving, caring, and devoted, but relatively few have the intensity of feeling for their children that Rabbi Nachum did. Incidentally, this is a trait which has filtered down to many of Rabbi Nachum's descendants.

All I can see is that if Rabbi Nachum's fatherly indulgence of his children was anything like my father's, then it was most abundant in love and devotion. I point this out because the story that follows is one that I heard from my father, and he related it with great admiration for Rabbi Nachum. This is the way my father told the story:

*A*fter Rabbi Nachum's demise, his wife would periodically visit his colleagues, fellow disciples of the Baal Shem Tov and the Maggid of Mezeitch, who helped support her.

One time, the rebbetzin visited Rebbe Baruch of Mezhibozh, the grandson of the Baal Shem Tov, and Rebbe Baruch asked her to relate some memoirs of her saintly husband.

After a few moments' thought, the rebbetzin arose and bid Rebbe Baruch farewell. In response to his astonishment at her abrupt departure, she said, "During the many years I shared with my husband, I gathered innumerable incidents of his greatness. At this very moment, not only can I not recall any of them, I cannot even retrieve his image. I take this as an indication that I do not belong here now."

Rebbe Baruch escorted the rebbetzin to her carriage. Just as the horses were about to move, she requested the driver to halt. She alighted from the carriage and said, "I recall one incident, which I have never revealed previously and would not do so now. However, since I cannot recall anything else, and this particular incident did come to my mind, I take this as an indication that this is what I am obliged to tell you.

"Rabbi Nachum and I lived in abject poverty. His entire day was spent in the study of Torah and in prayerful devotion.

"Rabbi Nachum had a pair of tefillin (phylacteries) which were very dear to him. The Scriptural portions contained in them had been written by Reb Ephraim, the scribe, whom the Baal Shem Tov considered to be second only to the Biblical scribes, Ezra and Nehemiah. These *tefillin were thus very special and most valuable. A wealthy member of the community had offered Rabbi Nachum 50 rubles for the tefillin, a sum which would have permitted our family to live in comfort for more than a year.*

"However, Rabbi Nachum had said he would never part with the tefillin. There were times when I pleaded with him to reconsider, such as when the children had not had any food for days, or when they were cold due to lack of proper clothing, and we had no wood for the fire. I would say, 'How can you be so heartless to your own children? They need food and clothing. For two rubles, you can buy a fine set of tefillin, and we can then afford the essentials of life with the remainder.' But I eventually learned that all my entreaties were in vain. The tefillin were not negotiable.

"We were also raising our orphaned niece, Malkele, who shared our meager existence. I would say to my husband, `When Malkele reaches marriageable age and needs a dowry, then you will sell the tefillin, won't you? After all, you are permitted to sell even a Torah to provide funds for a child to marry.' He would say that we would deal with that when the time came.

"One year as Rosh Hashanah approached, it was evident that there was going to be a dearth of esrogim for Succos. For whatever reason, no esrogim had arrived, and my husband was terribly upset over this. The mitzvah of esrog occurs but once a year, and to lose the opportunity to fulfill this mitzvah was inconceivable. He actually became depressed over this.

"On the way home from shul the morning of the day before Succos, my husband thought that from afar he saw a man carrying an esrog and lulav. Excitedly he ran after him and found this to be so. He asked the man how much he would take for the esrog and lulav, and the man responded, "Rabbi, this is not within your means. This is the only available esrog in the entire region, and is intended

for the wealthiest member of the community, who is paying 50 rubles for it.'

"Rabbi Nachum then remembered that he had been offered 50 rubles for his tefillin. He reasoned, 'I have already fulfilled the mitzvah of tefillin today. I will not need them again for nine days, until after Succos. But the mitzvah of esrog is one which I must fulfill tomorrow.' He then bade the man to wait a bit, ran off to the wealthy man, sold the tefillin for 50 rubles, and with the money purchased the esrog.

"When I returned home after trying to gather some scraps of food for the holiday, I found my husband beaming in euphoria. I inquired as to the reason for this joy, and whether perhaps he had acquired a few kopeks so that we could buy food for Yom Tov. But he just ignored my questions, and continued to behave as though he had found a fortune.

"I continued to press him for the reason for his joy, and he eventually told me that he had acquired an esrog. 'An esrog!' I exclaimed. 'Why, that is impossible! If there were an esrog available, its price would be prohibitive.' My husband reluctantly confessed that he had sold his tefillin in order to buy the esrog.

"As he said this, all the years of deprivation we had endured suddenly passed before my eyes. I saw the cold winters, when there was not a piece of firewood to mitigate the bitter frost, the children shivering in their tattered clothes. I remembered all those times the children were hungry and I had nothing to give them. But, no, he would not sell the tefillin then. Yet now he sells them for a piece of fruit that in eight days will be totally worthless! And what about Malkele's dowry? Malkele, my dead sister's child, whom we are responsible to raise and find a husband for. Whom would take her without a dowry? He sold Malkele's dowry for a piece of fruit that will be worthless in a week!

"This was more than I could bear. 'Where is the esrog?' I demanded. Silently, my husband pointed to the cupboard.

"In a fit of rage, I ran to the cupboard, grabbed the esrog, and with great force, threw it on the ground, smashing it into smithereens.

"My husband stood silent and motionless, his face ghastly pale. Two streams of tears trickled down his cheeks onto his beard.

"After a moment, he spoke. 'My precious tefillin I no longer have,' he said. 'The opportunity to fulfill the holy mitzvah of esrog on Succos I also do not have. Now Satan would wish that I lose my temper, shout at my wife, and ruin the spirit of joy on Yom Tov. That wish I will not grant him.' "

Rebbe Baruch listened, completely enraptured, and after a few moments of contemplation said, "Rebbetzin, Rabbi Nachum loved his children no less than you did. Their suffering certainly affected him as deeply as it did you, and his concern for Malkele's welfare also equaled yours. Yet I can grasp why he did not sell the tefillin throughout all those years of deprivation, and I can also grasp why he did sell them to acquire the esrog.

"But how on earth a human being can have so great a self-mastery, not to say even a single angry word upon an act which should have provoked intense rage, that only Rabbi Nachum could achieve."

Some people will say that the hero of the story is the Rabbi's wife, who put up with such severe deprivation for years. Some people who feel intensely for their children and empathize with their distress may feel very negatively toward Rabbi Nachum. As I mentioned, my father was capable of total self-effacement when it came to providing for the needs of his children. The suffering that Rabbi Nachum must have experienced when he was unable to provide for his children must have been very great. If we do not fully understand him, it is because we lack Rabbi Nachum's understanding of the inestimable value of a mitzvah. Both Rabbi Nachum and his rebbetzin are examples of a *living mesiras nefesh*.

Yet another example of *mesiras nefesh* for a mitzvah is illustrated by the following story.

O*ne year there was a dearth of esrogim (citrons for Succos), and the chassidic master, Rabbi Levi Yitzchak of Berditchev, was greatly distressed by the prospect that he would be unable to fulfill this precious mitzvah. He told his followers to be on the alert, and if they happened to come across an esrog, to obtain it for him regardless of the price. On the day before Succos a merchant who was traveling through Berditchev was observed to be in possession of an esrog and lulav, and the chassidim asked him to sell it to them for the tzaddik, and that money was no object. The merchant stated that he was wealthy and did not need the money, and had no intention of selling the esrog. They asked him to stay in Berditchev for the holiday so that the tzaddik could use the esrog, but the man stated that he was en route home to spend the holiday with his family. They convinced the man to meet with the tzaddik, and Rabbi Levi Yitzchak promised him that if he would remain in Berditchev for Succos, he would have a place adjoining him in Gan Eden in the eternal world. The man was no fool, and realized this was an opportunity that could not be lost, and agreed to stay in Berditchev.*

Shortly before the onset of the holiday, Rabbi Levi Yitzchak sent messengers all over town, instructing them not to allow this merchant entrance into their succos. At night, when the merchant wished to enter his host's succah for the meal, he was refused admission. Perplexed, he went to a neighbor, where he was again denied admission, and soon found out that due to the rabbi's decree, he would not be allowed into anyone's succah.

The enraged merchant confronted Rabbi Levi Yitzchak. "Is this how you repay a favor?" he asked. "I sacrificed being with my wife and children for the holiday in order to enable you to have the esrog, and you deny me the privilege of fulfilling the mitzvah of succah?" But Rabbi Levi Yitzchak stood fast. "I will not allow you to enter a succah in Berditchev unless you release me from the promise that you would join me in Paradise."

The merchant was bewildered. He had reluctantly agreed to remain in Berditchev only because of the unusual opportunity to be together with the tzaddik in Gan Eden, and now he was asked to surrender this. But what could he do? Unless he agreed to the tzaddik's terms, he would not be able to fulfill the mitzvah of succah. Reluctantly, he yielded and released the tzaddik from his promise.

Rabbi Levi Yitzchak welcomed the merchant into his succah and embraced him warmly. "My dear friend," he said, "you will indeed be with me in Gan Eden. You see, Gan Eden is not easily acquired, and although you had sacrificed being with your family for Yom Tov in order that I may be able to have an esrog, that was not yet sufficient for you to warrant Gan Eden. But when you had the mesiras nefesh to forfeit what was so valuable a prize for you in order to be able to fulfill the mitzvah of succah, you thereby merited Gan Eden."

Chassidic lore relates that the simchah of Rabbi Levi Yitzchak and the merchant on that remarkable Succos was unprecented. Everyone was alive and joyous. No one was martyred. But there was a true living mesiras nefesh.

Making G-d
Beloved

e recite the *Shema* daily, and declare, "You shall love G-d with all your heart, with all your soul, and with all your might." The Talmud states that to love G-d with all one's soul means that a person is prepared to give up one's life rather than to deny G-d. We are told that Rabbi Akiva recited the *Shema* when he was executed by the Romans, and stated that all his life he had looked forward to fulfilling the mitzvah of loving G-d with "all his soul."

The Talmud gives an additional interpretation to this verse of the *Shema* which confirms our understanding of *mesiras nefesh* as referring to a living *mesiras nefesh* as well as martyrdom.

The Talmud interprets the word *ve'ahavta* as meaning not only "you shall love," but also "you shall make beloved" (*Yoma* 86a). This is the concept of *kiddush HaShem* whereby one sanctifies the Divine Name by proper living rather than by martyrdom.

In the daily *Amidah* we say, "We shall sanctify Your Name in this world, just as the angels do in the celestial worlds, when they say, 'Holy, holy, holy.'" Yes, the way the angels sanctify G–d is by declaring His praises. Our task as humans is to sanctify His Name by our actions and behavior, over and above our praising Him in prayer. When we live according to true Torah values, we sanctify His Name on earth.

T he prototype for this type of kiddush HaShem is found in the Midrash. Rabbi Shimon ben Shatach bought a donkey from an Arab, and his students found a precious stone suspended from the donkey's neck. They told Rabbi Shimon of this windfall and said, "G–d has blessed you with wealth." Rabbi Shimon said, "I bought a mule. I did not buy a diamond," and returned the gem to its owner, who declared, "Blessed is the G–d of Shimon ben Shatach" (Devarim Rabbah 3).

The *kiddush HaShem* accomplished when one makes others give praise and honor to the G–d of Israel may surpass even that of martyrdom.

It is all the same whether it is a priceless gem or correcting an error of a few dollars made by the checkout clerk. Anytime a person demonstrates that one conducts his life on the principles of honesty, decency, and consideration, it is a *kiddush HaShem*. And when Torah-observant people demonstrate the incomparable beauty of Torah living, it is a *kiddush HaShem*.

In our Shabbos prayers we say, "Israel shall rest on this day, they who perform a *kiddush HaShem*." The Talmud states that just as G–d rested at the close of the week, having completed the work of Creation, so every Jew should consider everything as having been completed when Shabbos begins. There should be no carry-over from the workweek onto Shabbos, no worries about the job, the office, the debts, or whatever else character-izes the workweek. Without such carry-over, Shabbos becomes the ultimate day of rest, a true tranquillity, when one is not bur-dened by any of the stresses of the workweek. In absence of such stresses and worries, one can relate to loved ones and friends with a pleasant demeanor. All grudges, resentments, and pettiness are forgotten, and the atmosphere is indeed "a taste of *Olam Haba* (Paradise)." Shabbos becomes a day of spirituality, when a person feels himself drawn closer to G–d and to fellow men. It is truly a *Shabbos Shalom*, a day of peace. This quality of Shabbos observance will undoubtedly cause others to wish to share in this sublime delight. Living in a way that demonstrates the beauty of the Divine gift of Shabbos is a *kiddush HaShem*, and fulfills the commandment "to make G–d beloved."

Making G–d beloved can be of enormous benefit to a person. The *Midrash* states that the Torah and mitzvos were not given for G–d's benefit. G–d is All-perfect and needs nothing from us. Rather, they were given to us to refine us and make us better people (*Bereshis Rabbah* 44:1). The mitzvah of making G–d beloved can make us better.

The Baal Shem Tov said that the path to achieving love of G–d is by loving people. As in so many other cases, the reverse is also true: We can achieve love of people via love of G–d.

I wonder if we give enough serious consideration to the prayers and *berachos* we recite. For example, when we attend a wedding, the first *berachah* that is reciting after the wedding ring is given is "That G–d has created everything for His glory." Although we have heard this *berachah* countless times, have we ever paused to think why this is relevant at a wedding? It would certainly be appropriate to give the newlyweds a mes-sage that could strengthen their marriage, but how does the concept that G–d created the universe for His glory contribute to this?

Let us think for a moment. What would a marriage be like if both partners had as their primary consideration the increase of *kevod shamayim,* the glory of G–d? Their entire lives would be directed toward this goal. Their having children and raising them would be for this purpose, and their working together toward this common goal would bind them in a wondrous way. Things that might otherwise be irritants in a relationship would melt away in insignificance.

Granted, there are personal desires, both physical and emotional, that are part of a normal being. But how much emphasis should they receive? Obviously, if the marriage relationship is primarily to satisfy one's own needs, and the role of the partner is to provide for these needs, then any shortfall in such gratification can be a major irritant. If, however, the prime focus is *kevod shamayim,* then what might otherwise have become major frustrations may recede and can be easily overcome.

Yes, it is very nice for dinner to be ready on time, the table neatly set, and for everything to be in perfect order when the husband returns from work. But if this does not happen, has *kevod shamayim* really been affected? It should be obvious that the reaction to such an occurrence would be totally different if the purpose of the marriage is *kevod shamayim* rather than fulfillment of one's personal desires.

There are a myriad of factors that can impede the relationship between husband and wife, far too many to be enumerated. Even when a marriage begins with a strong bond of love, these irritants may cause a distancing, and may lead to varying degrees of domestic misunderstanding and strife. All this could be eliminated by a single factor — if the couple were single minded in the promotion of *kevod shamayim.*

This is why the first *berachah,* the first message to the newlyweds, is *shehakol bara lichvodo,* everything was created for the greater glory of G–d, and that is what the basis of the marriage should be. This is but a restatement of the *Shema*, to make G–d beloved. Dedication to making G–d beloved and increasing *kevod shamayim* can eliminate the multitude of would-be irritants that can undermine a love relationship.

In Judaism the term used for marriage is *kiddushin*, sanctity. We can see how this relates to *kiddush HaShem*, and how a living *mesiras nefesh*, by making one's personal needs secondary to *kevod shamayim,* can allow a marriage to flourish.

I cannot restrain myself from pointing out one aspect of making G–d beloved to which we can all contribute. It is a *kiddush HaShem* when any place that is associated with Torah and observance of mitzvos appears respectable, neat, and clean. Conversely, it is a serious dereliction in *kiddush HaShem* when such places are unkempt and unsightly. The Talmud, which is very careful with the expressions it uses, states that for a Torah scholar to be seen with stained clothes is a capital offense (*Shabbos* 114a). Anything that is associated with Torah should reflect cleanliness.

I was greatly distressed once, while walking through a very observant neighborhood in Israel, to note the litter on the streets. I was deeply hurt when I heard the comments of some passersby, who said, "*Aizeh lichluch*" (What filth!). Much harm is done to *kevod shamayim* when observant people are considered to be slovenly. When you enter the *succah* or put on the *tefillin,* I am sure that you have the *kavannah* (concentration) that you are fulfilling a mitzvah. Let me assure you that if you refrain from throwing a wrapper on the street or make the effort to pick up a piece of litter and put it in the waste basket, you are also fulfilling a very important mitzvah, of enhancing *kevod shamayim.*

You may remark that this latter digression is out of place in a treatise on *mesiras nefesh*. It is hardly *mesiras nefesh* to avoid littering or to pick up a piece of litter and deposit it in a trash can. My point is that developing and maintaining an attitude is that *kedushah* must be made attractive in every possible way, and dedicating oneself to the principle of "This is my G–d and I shall adorn Him" (*Exodus* 15:2) does require some sacrifice. Once this attitude is an integral part of one's personality, it may legitimately be considered *mesiras nefesh*.

The Ultimate Wisdom

The first words one utters on arising are *modeh ani lefonecha, melech* — I am grateful to You, O King, thereby acknowledging the sovereignty of G–d upon the first moment of consciousness of the day. Later, as we say the *Shema*, we formally accept the yoke of the Divine rule.

We pride ourselves on our intellect. After all, it is the genius of the human intellect that has given us the masterpieces of art and literature and the marvels of science. Who is not carried away by the majesty of Beethoven's symphonies or the depth of thought of the masters of literature? Only a fool could deny the miracles of modern science and medicine, the life-saving drugs and unprecedented surgical procedures, the ventures into outer space, and the magic of the computer. To take this immense genius and subjugate it to the Divine will, to the will of a Supreme Being Who is unseen and unknowable, is an act of faith and trust that is truly a *mesiras nefesh*.

Subjugating one's intellect to that of G–d may require a leap of faith, and for one who does so, this faith constitutes the principle of life itself. This was succinctly stated by the prophet, "And the righteous person shall live by his faith" (*Habbakuk* 2:4). Faith becomes life itself, and *mesiras nefesh* and subjugating one's will to that of G–d becomes possible, because to do otherwise would be taking leave of life.

The Talmud cites this verse from *Habbakuk* as being the foundation for the entire Torah, and that indeed, all 613 mitzvos are condensed into and contained within these few words (*Makkos* 24a). If we believe that G–d created the world, then there is a purpose to Creation, and in a purposeful world there is a goal and purpose for every individual. Denial of Creation, seeing the world as having evolved spontaneously from primordial matter makes existence essentially meaningless, and ultimately leads to hedonism. If there is no design and purpose to life, there is no reason why one should simply not maximize the pleasures of life. "Eat, drink, and be merry, for tomorrow you die."

The choice is thus between assuming that life is goal-directed, which places a burden of responsibility upon a person, or that it is an accident of nature, which allows one to be carefree and indulgent. One's judgment process is profoundly affected by bias, and a judge who has been bribed cannot be objective. The person who must judge whether to accept or renounce faith is bribed by the fact that acceptance is burdensome, whereas rejection of faith leaves one free to indulge all one's desires. Overcoming the temptation for a life free of moral restraints and dictates requires *mesiras nefesh*, and the person who subordinates himself to the will of G–d is making an enormous sacrifice which is indeed a *mesiras nefesh*.

The human mind is inquisitive, and it only natural to wish to know why. What is the reason behind what we are told to do?

This is a desire we must essentially surrender when we defer to the Superior wisdom. While we may be able to see how many of the mitzvos are advantageous to us, we cannot aspire to know their true reason. Inasmuch as the Torah is the Divine wisdom, we cannot grasp the wisdom of G–d anymore than we can grasp His essence. Both are equally unknowable.

The Talmud points out that King Solomon, the wisest of all men, relied on his enormous wisdom and sought to apply it to the performance of mitzvos. Thus, while the Torah said that a king should not take many wives because they might lead him astray, Solomon thought, "I am not in danger of being led astray." His assuming he understood the reason for the mitzvah led Solomon to assume this dictum did not apply to him, and this led to his downfall (*Sanhedrin* 21b).

The one mitzvah in the Torah which defies all understanding is the ritual of the red heifer (*Numbers* ch.19). This mitzvah is introduced with the words, "This is the law of the Torah." The commentaries explain that the principle of the mitzvah of the red heifer, i.e., that it is something beyond the grasp of the human intellect, is the law of the entire Torah. Even when we think we understand the purpose of a mitzvah, and even when we can see its palpable benefit, we must observe it as though it were completely beyond our comprehension, and do so solely because it is the Divine wish, dictated by a Supreme wisdom to which we must defer.

Yet there are those who repeat Solomon's mistake and insist their understanding a Torah command is a prerequisite to observing it. It should be recognized that if one observes only that which one understands, one is essentially worshipping himself and his own intellect rather than worshipping G–d.

It is related that a *tzaddik* gave a poor person *tzedakah,* then returned and gave him *tzedakah* a second time. He explained, "When I saw this man in tattered clothes and obviously in hunger, my heart ached for him. I gave him money to ease my own discomfort, and I would have done so even if there were no mitzvah of *tzedakah.* After my own distress at his plight was appeased, I was able to give him *tzedakah* as fulfillment of the mitzvah."

While it is certainly commendable to give *tzedakah* for whatever reason, the point made by this *tzaddik* is that following the dictates of one's heart and intellect does not constitute Divine service. It is only when we defer to the Divine wisdom and set aside the dictates of our heart and mind that it can be considered *avodas Hashem,* serving G–d.

Indeed, the cardinal sin of *avodah zarah,* idolatry, consists essentially of following one's own wishes, rather than deferring to a higher wisdom. Scripture relates the indulgence of the Israelites in *avodah zarah,* and we may wonder how previous generations that were so much wiser than us could have believed in pagan idols. The Talmud explains that the Israelites never believed, even for a moment, that these idols had any substance. Rather, because they wished to gratify their own desires, and wished to do so with the approval of an authority, they created or accepted religions which would allow them to institute their own laws and attribute them to a superior being (*Sanhedrin* 63b). *Avodah zarah* was nothing other than the worship of one's own mind, projected onto an idol.

We begin the Passover *seder* with the child asking a number of questions: Why do we eat matzah and *marror?* Why this and why that? The father replies, "We were slaves unto Pharaoh." *Masseh Nissim* explains the answer as, "When we were slaves to Pharaoh, a temporal ruler, we did as he commanded, and it was not our prerogative to ask for an explanation for his edicts. Now that we were liberated by G–d and accepted Him as our Sovereign, we do as He commands, and likewise, it is not necessary for us to know the reasons for everything.

The proper performance of mitzvos thus requires setting aside our desire to understand, and deferring to the wisdom of G–d. When we do so day in and day out, we are truly embracing a *living mesiras nefesh.*

In All
Your Ways

The totality of a *living mesiras nefesh* must be comparable to the totality of the *mesiras nefesh* of martyrdom. Just as there is no partial surrendering of one's life in the latter, so should the *living mesiras nefesh* be a total commitment.

Some people may think that there are major Torah requirements which are of great importance, and minor ones which can be considered trivia, and with which one may take liberties. This attitude betrays a lack of *mesiras nefesh*. Totality means just that: There is nothing in Torah observance that can be considered trivia. This is clearly stated in the Talmud: "Be as meticulous about a minor mitzvah as a major one, since you are not in the position to measure their worth" (*Ethics of the Fathers* 2:1). The *Midrash* states that the true test of a person's greatness lies not in his conduct on major issues, but how he handles minor issues (*Shemos Rabbah* 2:3). This explains an enigmatic statement of the *Maggid* of Koznitz who was a noted Talmudic scholar. He was asked, "Why do you go to the Rebbe of Mezeritch? With your voluminous knowledge of Torah, what is there that you expect to learn from him?"

The *Maggid* replied, "I go to Mezeritch to observe how the Rebbe ties his shoes." By that he meant that the measure of a *tzaddik* is not how he performs the mitzvos, but how he conducts himself in the trivia of everyday life. A *living mesiras nefesh* requires a literal understanding of the verse "Know G-d in *all* your ways" (*Proverbs* 6:3), and a commitment of every facet of one's life to the will of G-d.

We have appliances that can operate on either "manual" or "automatic." While automatic may be far simpler, manual gives a person moment-to-moment control. We can operate our lives by either manual or automatic. In order to make certain that everything we do is dedicated to fulfilling the Divine will, we must operate on manual, because only in this way can we have the requisite alertness and *kavannah* (concentration and intention).

At the very least, performance of mitzvos should not be automatic. The Talmud admonishes us, "Do not allow your prayer to be routine, but rather sincere supplication before G-d" (*Ethics of the Fathers* 2:18). We would be less than truthful if we claimed anything near perfection in this regard. Many people who pray daily would have to admit that their *kavannah* in prayer is often rather weak, and that at times they essentially go through the motions of verbalizing and swaying, although their thoughts may be elsewhere.

It is indeed commendable that we kiss the *mezuzah*, but too often this is a perfunctory act, with little thought about the contents of the *mezuzah*. The writing in the *mezuzah* declares the unity of G-d and *kabbalas ol*, acceptance of the yoke of His sovereignty, which constitutes the *living mesiras nefesh*. There is little value in kissing the *mezuzah* if this is not an expression of affection for G-d. I saw the Rebbe of Klausenberg pause at the door, place his hand on the *mezuzah*, close his eyes and meditate a few moments. He did not kiss his fingers as is the customary practice, but his meditation on the *mezuzah* was far more meaningful.

Not only should our mitzvos be performed with *kavannah*, but everything we do should be with the *kavannah* that it is directed to the Divine will. Sleeping because one is tired is automatic. Lying down to rest with the thought, "I must restore my energy so that I can do that which G-d requires of me," is manual. Eating to satisfy hunger is an automatic response. Eating so that one may have the energy to live and perform mitzvos is manual. In order to help us dedicate our eating to the Divine service, our sages formulated *berachos* (blessings) before partaking of food. Their intent was to alert us that in contrast to other creatures, we should not eat solely to satisfy our appetites, but for loftier reasons as well. But alas! Too often we rattle off the *berachos* without adequate thought to the meaning of the words, and we fail to sublimate our eating.

*I*n a dream the Baal Shem Tov was shown who his neighbor in Gan Eden (Paradise) would be. His curiosity aroused, the Baal Shem Tov traveled to the village where this man lived, and was surprised to find that he was an unlearned person who did not show any evidence of special piety. The one thing that the Baal Shem Tov did notice was that the man ate more than usual and spent much time in physical fitness exercises, so that he appeared very strong and robust.

"Why all the interest in developing physical strength?" the Baal Shem Tov asked.

The man responded, "I remember hearing stories about Jews in the time of the Inquisition who were tortured until they succumbed and denied G-d. Just let anyone try that with me," he said. He picked up a thick branch and broke it in two as if it were a toothpick. "If anyone theatens me with torture unless I deny my G-d, they'll be sorry they started up with me."

The Baal Shem Tov said, "Now I understand why this man deserves a rich reward in Gan Eden. Every single bite of food he takes is for the purpose of kiddush HaShem."

A rabbi once lodged at an inn, and he saw the innkeeper put on his *talis* (prayer shawl) for the morning prayers. Just then a customer came in for a quart of beer. The innkeeper drew a quart of beer from the barrel, but the customer began haggling over the price, whereby the innkeeper returned the beer to the barrel, excused himself, and went on to finish his prayers. To the bewildered rabbi he explained, "When the customer asked for a quart of beer, this gave me the opportunity to perform the mitzvah of giving him an honest measure (*Deuteronomy* 25:15), and I will do a mitzvah at anytime. But haggling over the price is merely business, and I don't do business before I finish praying."

Yes, transacting with customers can be a mitzvah if one bears in mind that by dealing fairly and honestly one is fulfilling the dictates of the Torah.

Operating on manual may appear to be very demanding, but if it is a labor of love as it should be, it is really not burdensome. The *Maggid* of Koznitz was sickly and at times had to be carried on a couch to the *shul* because he was too weak to walk. However, once he entered the *shul*, he would leap from the couch, run to the *amud* (lectern) and pray with a fervor and gesticulations that would be exhausting for a person of good health and strength.

The incomparable *Maggid* of Dubno explained the verse "It is not Me that you have called upon, O Jacob, if you are weary in My service, O Israel" (*Isaiah* 43:22) with a parable. A diamond merchant was awaiting delivery of a parcel of merchandise. When he answered the door, he saw the messenger dripping with perspiration, who remarked, "That was a really big load I carried." The merchant remarked, "I am sorry. You must have mixed up your deliveries. My parcel is very small and could hardly exhaust you." Similarly, if one is made weary by the service of G-d, something must have gone wrong. A sincere service out of profound love for G-d is not exhausting.

It is important to keep oneself always on the alert, because it is so easy to slip into automatic. The physical body prefers comfort, and operating on automatic is certainly easier. The *Midrash* states that G-d brought all the animals before Adam to be named, and Adam gave each one the name that described its essence. "And what will your name be?" G-d asked. "My name will be Adam," man answered, "because I was formed from *adamah* (earth)." The Alter of Slobodka explains that Adam gave himself this name to serve as a reminder so that he would always be conscious of the earthly component of his being, and thereby be alert to the gravitational force that draws him back to his physical source, rather than allow him to soar to spiritual heights.

The ethicist, Rabbi Leib Chasman, cites the admonition of the prophet, "An ox knows its master, and the mule recognizes the feeding trough of its owner, but My people does not know Me" (*Isaiah* 1:3), and he points out that when a human being is not aware of G-d he not only descends to the level of a brute beast, but falls even beneath that. A person is thus at either extreme: When he overcomes his resistance and acknowledges G-d as his Sovereign, he is superior to angels, since the latter have no resistances to overcome. Angels stand in the imminent presence of G-d and are not inhibited from recognizing Him as is man, hence there is no virtue in their being aware of Him, whereas for man this is a virtue. But when man fails to overcome his resistance and denies G-d, he is even lower than beasts, who do recognize their master.

The very first paragraph of the *Shulchan Aruch* tells us to always view ourselves as being in the presence of G-d because the way we would behave in the presence of the King is certainly much different than if we were unobserved. This is a principle of *living mesiras nefesh*.

Acknowledging Gratitude

The association of the term *mesiras nefesh* with martyrdom may lead us to believe that *living mesiras nefesh* applies only to heroic acts of surrender. The fact is that *living mesiras nefesh* can manifest itself in many activities which are quite commonplace.

Some people find it very difficult to express gratitude, and even to *feel* gratitude. Acknowledging a kindness from someone may cause one to feel obligated and beholden to that person, and if these feelings are unpleasant, people may defend themselves against them, albeit unconsciously, by denying that they received a favor. This tendency seems to be almost innate, as it can be observed in small children who have not yet had an opportunity to become worldly or sophisticated. A five-year-old may receive a gift or a piece of candy, and when mother says, "Say 'thank you' to the nice man," the child may respond with a grunt and a defiant twist of his shoulders, indicating that he is not about to acknowledge the favor.

The Talmud tells us that Moses admonished the Israelites for being ingrates, and *Tosafos* explains that their refusal to feel gratitude was because they did not wish to feel obligated to G-d (*Avodah Zarah* 5a). If this is so in relationship to G-d, how much more so is it when one receives a favor from another person, where the feeling of indebtedness may be thought of as demeaning.

Overcoming the resistance to feeling and expressing gratitude may require much effort, and this constitutes *mesiras nefesh*. Achievement of this has been made somewhat easy for us by virtue of our prayers. There is less resistance to acknowledging a kindness from G-d than from another human being, because it is a lesser blow to one's ego to feel indebted to G-d than to another person. When we repeatedly express our thanks to G-d in our prayers or *berachos* (blessings) and hear ourselves say "thank you" to Him, it lessens our resistance to saying the same words to another human being.

We have seen that a *living mesiras nefesh* is in fact beneficial and is ultimately self-preserving rather than self-sacrificing. The acknowledgment of gratitude is no exception. Some people are fiercely independent, refusing to accept legitimate help because of their reluctance to feel indebted. I know of one aggressive business executive who refused to remain in the hospital intensive care unit following a heart attack because he could not tolerate being in a situation where others were looking after him. He disconnected his monitor and intravenous and left the hospital. Such people make life much more difficult for themselves than it should be, as they assume unnecessary burdens for which they could have received help.

The importance of feeling and expressing gratitude should be evident from the fact that the very first words that should appear on our lips when we wake up in the morning are *modeh ani*, I thank You, I am grateful. It should also be evident that although the *shaliach tzibbur* (cantor) may represent the congregants in reciting the *Amidah* (*Shemoneh Esrei* prayer), this does not apply to *Modim*, the expression for gratitude, which each person must say of himself. Indeed, while formal prayer is of rabbinical origin, the *bentsching* (Grace After Meals) is of Scriptural origin, further indicating the central role of acknowledging gratitude in Torah living.

One of the most elaborate mitzvah rituals is that of *bikkurim*, bringing the first-ripened fruit as an offering to the Sanctuary. The Talmud describes in detail the pomp and beauty that accompanied the performance of this mitzvah. Although employees are not permitted to say the full-length prayers while working, and are required to say only an abridged version in order that they do not impinge on their employers' time, an exception is made for *bikkurim*, where they may interrupt their work in order to greet people who brought the offering to the Sanctuary. Why this special dispensation? Because *bikkurim* is an expression of gratitude, and this is of such great importance that it overrides other considerations.

Let me digress a bit to point out that one of the benefits we accrue from prayer is that it facilitates salutary behavior. As we have just seen, there may be resistance to acknowledging a favor from another person, if one wishes to avoid the feeling of being beholden to others. Although this resistance may apply even to Divine favors, there is less resistance in expressing gratitude toward G-d than to another human being. Hence, if we get into the habit of saying "thank you" to G-d, the words might come off our tongues just a bit easier when we relate to other people.

By the same token, there may also be some hesitance in declaring feelings of affection to other people. Is it not strange that during courtship while people often have no difficulty in expressing their feeling for one another, yet it is possible that during the next 60 years of marriage, they do not express these sentiments even once? Perhaps our saying *ve'ahavta* three times each day, declaring our love for G-d, may make it a bit easier for us to say these words to those we love.

And finally, our confessing our sins and our regret for having done wrong at various points in our prayers should lower our resistance toward admitting our mistakes instead of defending them. Three magic words: " I was wrong." I wonder how many divorces might have been avoided and how much devastation resulting from disintegration of families might have been eliminated if people had only said the phrase, "I'm sorry for what I said/did" a bit more often. Again, hearing ourselves say these words in our prayers and thinking about what they mean should facilitate our saying them to other people.

Let us return to gratitude. The fact that *hakoras hatov*, acknowledging the good done to us, receives so much attention in our ethical writings is not only indicative of its importance in character development, but also of the enormous effort that must be exerted in its achievement. This qualifies it as a component of living *mesiras nefesh*.

We must take this one step further. Not only should we be grateful to G-d for His kindnesses, but we must also accept His forgiveness for the wrongs we have done, once we have done *teshuvah*; i.e., recognized our mistakes, resolved never to repeat them, and taken appropriate precautions that we do not succumb to temptation again. Proper *teshuvah* is more than just remorse. It requires a sincere soul-searching to identify the shortcomings in our spirituality that allowed the transgression to occur, and then to eliminate these character defects. Once we have done proper *teshuvah*, we must accept Divine forgiveness. Retaining guilt is essentially a denial of G-d's forgiveness, of which we have been repeatedly assured.

The Talmud states that the destruction of the Sanctuary and our exile from our homeland was the consequence of the sin of the spies, who caused the Israelites to doubt that G-d would fulfill his promise to give them the land of Canaan. The night that the Israelites wept upon hearing the report of the spies was *Tishah B'Av* (the ninth day of Av), and this day was designated for perpetual mourning, as both the first and second Temples were destroyed on *Tishah B'Av* (*Taanis* 29a).

Sforno comments that the reason the Israelites doubted that they would conquer Canaan is because they felt guilty about having engaged in idol worship during their stay in Egypt. The spies' report about the formidable strength of the Canaanites made the Israelites realize that conquest of the land was possible only by a Divine miracle, and their guilt made them feel unworthy of Divine favor.

But is it not only proper for a person to feel guilty about a transgression? The answer is, yes, but only until one has done *teshuvah*. When the Israelites had been assured by Moses that G-d would give them the land of Canaan because he had forgiven their transgressions in Egypt, as was indicated by the miraculous dividing of the waters of the Red Sea, there was no ground for retention of guilt.

Let us just digest this for a moment. The greatest calamity that has befallen our people throughout history resulted not because of a sin as grievous as worship of the golden calf, but, according to Sforno, their inability to accept that G-d had forgiven them.

The *yetzer hara* (evil inclination) is shrewd and cunning, and will attempt to achieve its purpose to destroy a person by any and all methods. It may entice a person to sin, and may deter him from doing *teshuvah*. However, if a person has done *teshuvah*, the *yetzer hara* may don a cloak of piety and try to convince the person, "You are evil. You have not been forgiven. Your *teshuvah* is inadequate. G-d had turned away from you." A person can be paralyzed by such misguided piety.

Allow me another digression to point out one reason why a person may have difficulty in accepting forgiveness. We can have a thorough understanding only of things with which we have had some experience. For example, we may use words such as "eternity" or "infinity," but we really have no understanding of these concepts, since we have never come into actual contact with anything that had no beginning and no end or was limitless. While we do use these terms, they are rather meaningless words.

Much the same may be true of forgiveness. Unless we have had the experience of totally forgiving someone who has offended us, and totally removed all traces of resentment from our hearts, we may have great difficulty in accepting Divine forgiveness. Therefore, if you find yourself still feeling guilty after you feel you have done adequate teshuvah, I suggest you think of someone against whom you bear a grudge. Now find it in your heart to totally forgive that person. You may be surprised to find that your feelings of guilt disappear. This may have been part of the intent of the Talmudic statement that G-d forgives those who forgive others (Megillah 28a).

We must believe that G-d loves us and wishes to give us of His endless bounty. Our expectations should be that good things will happen, and we should not anticipate misfortune. By accepting G-d's forgiveness we can free ourselves of the crushing force of guilt. We should acknowledge G-d's kindness and mercy, and be grateful to Him for them.

Regret Is Not Enough

As mere mortals, we are fallible and we make mistakes. We have been given a Divine gift of *teshuvah,* and we have been assured that once we have done *teshuvah,* our sins are totally erased, leaving no trace whatever, "like a fog that has cleared." However, this is contingent on our doing a *thorough teshuvah.*

We may indeed deeply regret having done something wrong, and we may even make a sincere resolution to never repeat the misdeed. Commendable as this may be, it is still not adequate to completely remove every vestige of this sin. The latter requires a *teshuvah* so complete, Rambam says, that G-d Himself will testify that the person will never repeat the act (*Rambam, Hilchos Teshuvah* 2:3).

Various commentaries raise a question about Rambam's description of proper *teshuvah*. Inasmuch as we believe that in matters of moral behavior man has total freedom to act, and G-d does not intervene to stop someone from committing a sin, how can G-d testify as to a person's moral behavior in the future? A person has total freedom to choose between right and wrong, at any moment, and we are told that the High Priest Yochanan, after 70 years of devout dedication to Torah, defected to the Sadducees. If G-d testifies that a person will never commit a particular sin, this in effect deprives him of the freedom to do so, which is incompatible with one of the principle of faith.

The answer to this question came to me from a totally unexpected source. A recovering alcoholic who was sober for over 20 years said, "The man I once was, drunk; and the man I once was, will drink again. Today I do not drink because my character has undergone a change. If I should go back to being the person I once was, I will drink again. At one time in my life I was sober, and it was that sober person that began drinking. I cannot go back to being that sober person and expect anything other than a repetition of what happened."

At that point I had a flash of insight into what Rambam was describing as adequate *teshuvah*. A sin does not occur in a vacuum. It occurs only in a person who is in such a state where he is capable of committing that sin. If he wishes to avoid repeating that sin, he must elevate himself to a level of spirituality where that behavior is totally foreign to him. If he acquires that level of spirituality, then his *teshuvah* is complete.

Of course, there is no guarantee that one will remain at a particular level of spirituality. It is possible that a person may suffer spiritual deterioration, and fall to a level at which he may sin again. Rambam does not mean that G-d will testify that the person will never sin again, because that would indeed eliminate freedom of choice. What G-d can testify is that the person has achieved a high-enough level of spirituality at which he will not repeat his sinful behavior, and indeed, if this level is maintained, he will not sin again.

Teshuvah is thus more than regret or resolution. It is nothing less than an overhaul of one's personality.

That this is the true essence of *teshuvah* is further supported by the formula for confession of sins cited in the *Jerusalem Talmud* (*Yoma* 8:7), where the penitent person states, "I sinned because I was on the wrong path." Sinful behavior is more than an isolated incident or series of incidents. Rather, it is symptomatic of a faulty path in life or a particular life-style which the person has adopted, and which he must abandon if he wishes to avoid recurrence of sin.

However, no one wishes to make a radical change in lifestyle, because this is distinctly uncomfortable. Regretting a particular act and resolving not to repeat it is not too formidable a task, but recognizing that an improper act is indicative of a deficiency in spirituality, and that one must advance spiritually to a state where that behavior is no longer feasible, is indeed a major challenge, and this calls for *mesiras nefesh*.

The degree of *mesiras nefesh* that is necessary to undertake a personality overhaul requires a strong motivation, because one may encounter intense resistance. As I mentioned in the introduction, the recovering alcoholic is motivated when he finally comes to the awareness that his life is a shambles, and furthermore, each time he has tried to abstain without changing his character, he ended up with a relapse. Having exhausted all other options, he finally surrenders to the need to make significant changes in his life-style. This is not as easy in the non-alcoholic who may lack palpable evidence that he is on a wrong path, and he may treat his misdeeds as isolated incidents which can be dealt with on their own, without undergoing a major character change. The *mussar* authorities state that the only way one can come to a true realization of one's status is to dedicate oneself to serious study of *mussar,* which can reveal the true state of one's being and motivate a person to take personal inventory and institute the proper changes.

There is great reward in the *mesiras nefesh* of *teshuvah,* and this is consistent with our thesis that *mesiras nefesh* is not really a sacrifice. The Talmud states that sincere *teshuvah,* done out of love for G-d, converts sins into merits (*Yoma* 86b), and that the place occupied by someone who has done *teshuvah* is beyond reach of a person who has never sinned (*Berachos* 34b).

Rabbi Schneur Zalman speaks of the relationship between man and G-d as being via a connecting rope, as it is written, "Jacob is the 'rope' of G-d's portion" (*Deuternomy* 32:9). When a person sins, he breaks this connection, and when he does *teshuvah,* the connection is restored. If we think of the connection as being a rope, then a sin is a break in the rope, and when one does *teshuvah,* the two ends at the break are tied together. When one ties a broken rope, it is shortened, which means that the person who does *teshuvah* has a closer connection to G-d than someone who has never sinned, whose rope is at its original length.

The Talmud states that by embracing the Torah's laws, one can become "a partner with G-d in the work of creation" (see, for example, Shabbos 10a and 119b). In describing the creation of man, the Torah states, "G-d said, 'Let us make man'" (*Genesis* 1:26). Various explanations are given for the expression "let *us,*" since obviously G-d created man singlehandedly.

The Baal Shem Tov explained that all other living things were created in a state of completion. Animals are complete at birth, and need only grow in size, but do not undergo any radical change. Even those animals that do undergo a metamorphosis have these changes inherent in their genes, and can do nothing to bring them about. Angels, on the other hand, do not grow or undergo any changes whatsoever. Man is unique, in that he is created in a state of incompletion, essentially an animal in nature, and by his own efforts must become master over his animalistic drives, and exercise the potentials of his spirit to make himself the unique being that he is supposed to be.

If G-d had created man as a fully developed spiritual being, he would essentially be another angel. G-d's intent, however, was not to have more angels, but humans who would develop themselves to their state of completion. Thus, G-d and man *together* create the final product: G-d gives man the potential, and man must develop it. Man is therefore indeed, as the Talmud says, a partner with G-d in the work of creation.

Man becomes the crowning jewel of creation when he strives to overcome his imperfections, and this is what *teshuvah* is all about.

Beware the Excesses

While *mesiras nefesh* generally involves some kind of deprivation, restriction of comfort, and what may be considered to be sacrifices, the converse is not necessarily true. I.e., not every sacrifice, even when made with good intentions, is commendable *mesiras nefesh*.

Moses began his review of the mitzvos with the admonition, "Do not add to the mitzvos which G-d has given you" (*Deuteronomy* 4:2). We are commanded to adhere to the instructions which the Torah authorities give us; hence, we observe Chanukah and Purim and a number of precautionary measures of rabbinic origin. However, on our own we are not permitted to add to what the

Torah says, and by the same token, to what *halachah* pre-
scribes.

Some practices can be either good or bad, depending on circumstances. For example, the Talmud states that a person who
fasts as an act of penance is praiseworthy, yet the Talmud also
states that a person who fasts is a sinner (*Nedarim* 10a). The
obvious question is: "Is fasting good or bad?" and the answer is,
"It depends." There are some situations in which fasting is commendable and others when it is not. This distinction should be
made by a Torah authority, a person well grounded in *halachah*
and *mussar*, who can analyze a situation and decide whether or
not one should fast.

Indulgence in material pleasures is antithetical to spirituality. Yet, the Talmud states that it is blameworthy for a person
to make a vow to restrict himself from permissible material
pleasures. "Is it not sufficient for you what the Torah has forbidden, that you add on new prohibitions?" (*Jerusalem
Talmud, Nedarim* 9:1). The Talmud encourages a person who
made such a vow to have it annulled.

One of the greatest mitzvos is giving *tzedakah*, yet even here
the Talmud places a limit on how much *tzedakah* a person is
permitted to disperse. Under most circumstances one is not to
exceed 20% of one's income: Greater disbursements may result
in compromising one's economic security, to the point where
one may become dependent on others.

One of the worst transgressions is speaking *lashon hara*, and
the great sage of the previous generation, the Chafetz Chaim,
essentially dedicated his life's work to eradicating *lashon hara*.
But suppose that one learns that an acquaintance is planning to
enter a business venture with a partner, and one knows that the
latter is an unscrupulous person who has brought others to ruin.
This is not the time to be concerned with *lashon hara*, says the
Chafetz Chaim. Rather, one must observe the Torah requirement to protect others from harm, and must inform his friend
about the proposed partner's dishonesty.

The Talmud refers to the concept of "misguided piety," and gives an example of a man who refuses to save a woman from drowning because he wishes to observe the injunction against coming into physical contact with a strange woman (*Sotah* 21b). There can also be misguided piety when one practices self-sacrifice.

Everyone is required to observe that which is written in the *Shulchan Aruch*. If a person wishes to go beyond what the *Shulchan Aruch* requires, he should seek an opinion from a competent *halachic* authority as to whether this is advisable.

One man was ordered to drink water on Yom Kippur in order to protect him from a potentially dangerous reaction to a medication he was taking. Inasmuch as it was not necessary for him to eat, he wished to have the liquid intake accomplished by intravenous fluids, which would allow him to fast on Yom Kippur, and he asked me whether this was appropriate. I consulted the noted Torah scholar, Rabbi Yaakov Kamenetzky, who said, "Heaven forbid! If the doctors have ordered him to drink, he is required to drink, because the Torah demands this, and one must not try to circumvent Torah requirements."

Yes, there were exceptions. There were great *tzaddikim* who fasted regularly and who took upon themselves various stringent practices which are not required by *halachah*. But such practices are not for you and me, and if we feel inclined to exceed *halachah* for established customs, we should do so only upon the ruling of a *halachic* authority.

The tzaddik of Sanz was known for his incomparable tzedakah. He not only gave away every cent he had to the poor, but if he could not fall asleep at night, he would search the house for money, assuming that it was the possession of money that was disturbing his peace. His kiddush cup and the Chanukah menorah were always in the pawnshop, because he pawned these to give the money to the poor. His son, the Rabbi of Shinova, a tzaddik in his own right, said, "My father had his reasons for doing so. I abide by the halachah to give 20 percent of my income to tzedakah. A friend of mine tried to emulate my father, and had reason to regret it."

The Rabbi of Ropschitz cited the Talmud which states that if a person recites chapter 144 of *Psalms* three times a day, he is deserving of *Gan Eden* (Paradise). "Then what about someone who recites this Chapter four times a day?" asked the Rabbi. "He is even more deserving, is he not?" The Rabbi answered, "No, he is a fool. If there were virtue in reciting it four times a day, the Talmud would have said so. If the Talmud says three times a day, one should not try to improve upon it."

As precious as the mitzvah of eating in the *succah* is, the *Shulchan Aruch* states that if it is raining to the degree that eating in the *succah* is distressing, one should eat in the house. Furthermore, anyone who eats in the *succah* under distressing conditions is a simpleton (*Orach Chaim* 639:7).

These examples should suffice to clarify the concept of *mesiras nefesh*. We are to have *mesiras nefesh* in observing the will of G-d, which is expressed in *halachah*. Going beyond *halachah* may be doing one's own will rather than the will of G-d, and this is not *mesiras nefesh*.

It's About Time

f people were asked, "what is the major industry in the United States?" some people may say the manufacture of automobiles, and others may say the health care field, but both are wrong. The major industry in the United States is that of providing for leisure-time activities: radio, television, theater, vacations, the various sports, and other diversionary activities. These by far dwarf all the others.

We live in an age of unprecedented technological marvels with time-saving devices that our ancestors could not have imagined in their wildest fantasies: America to Europe in several hours rather than weeks or months; fax machines and e-mail that deliver messages in seconds instead of days; microwave ovens that cook in minutes instead of hours. Add to these the shorter workweek and the prolongation of life beyond the retirement age, and you have unoccupied time in quantities never previously imagined.

But alas! Many people do not know what to do with this available time, and they are confronted with the challenge of intolerable boredom. I have had patients who never abused alcohol until they were "blessed" with free time which became their undoing. And so to save people from alcoholism, other addictions, and even suicidal depression, a whole new industry has arisen to help people "kill time."

Is this not the worst type of insanity? If someone were to be seen throwing money into the ocean, he would certainly be certified as mentally ill and institutionalized. Yet, money is a replaceable commodity, whereas time is the most unrenewable commodity we have. A moment wasted is irretrievable, and since life is finite, a wasted moment is an irreplaceable loss. This notwithstanding, people may sit in front of their television sets for hours, and even if what they watch is not morally objectionable, it is generally nothing but a time-occupying activity, to prevent their suffering the torment of boredom.

Swimming against the current is difficult. It takes a great deal of effort and fortitude to defy one's environment. We may be unwittingly pulled along with the mainstream. After all, many types of leisure activities are not explicitly forbidden by *halachah,* so why not partake of them?

Do not misunderstand me. Some amount of relaxation and diversion is necessary for optimal functioning and is therefore commendable, but when this necessary quantity is exceeded and one overindulges in leisure activities, it is spiritually damaging.

We were put on earth to do the Divine will as it is set forth in the Torah. We are workers who have been assigned a job. Just as an employer provides a brief coffee break because this is beneficial for work performance, so is the appropriate amount of diversion beneficial for completion of our mission. But just as exceeding the allotted time for the coffee break is essentially a misuse of the time for which one is being paid, so is the waste of time in excessive leisure activities a dereliction in performance of our mission.

There is an abundance of Torah activities which can occupy a person's time, whether it is the study of Torah or performance of the mitzvos. *Bitul Torah*, allowing precious time to be wasted, is a grave transgression. One's time should be spent in attending to the family's material and emotional needs, earning a livelihood, support of friendship, and assisting with communal responsibilities. Judicious diversion and relaxation is essential for good health, but inasmuch as "judicial" is a matter of opinion, we should be cautious not to rationalize and consider what is actually indulgence as being "judicious."

Our great personalities were paragons as guardians of time. The Rabbi of Gur once sent his watch for repair because it lost a minute every three weeks, and for him this was an intolerable inaccuracy. Rabbi Elimelech of Lizhensk writes that when one lies in bed unable to fall asleep, one should think about his belief in the unity of G-d as expressed in the *Shema*, and his willingness to give up his life if he were threatened with death unless he repudiated his belief in G-d. In view of the fact that meditating about a mitzvah is meritorious, one converts what would otherwise be wasted moments in the performance of a mitzvah. Not even the minutes elapsing while falling asleep should be allowed to go to waste.

*A*fter the close of Yom Kippur, one of the older yeshivah students in B'nei Brak visited the Chazon Ish and inquired how he was feeling following the fast.

"Let me tell you a true story," the Chazon Ish replied. "When Reb Itzel of Volozhin chose the Netziv (Rabbi Naftali Zvi Berlin) as a husband for his daughter, many of his friends and family were disappointed, because the Netziv had succeeded in concealing his genius from everyone. They openly criticized Reb Itzel for taking a son-in-law who *they felt was no more than an average scholar, and whom was nonetheless destined to succeed him as dean of the yeshivah of Volozhin.*

"Reb Itzel did not respond to these remarks, but one Yom Kippur, after the fast was over, he asked the well-wishers who had come to visit him to accompany him. He led them down a long corridor and finally into a small room, where the young Netziv was diligently studying the Talmud. 'You should eat something after the fast,' Reb Itzel said to his son-in-law.

"'I've already eaten,' the young Netziv replied.

"Reb Itzel turned to the group. 'You see, you have time to spend on greetings after the close of the fast, whereas he has already broken his fast and is engaged in Torah study. He does not waste a moment, and that is why I chose him.'"

The Chazon Ish then said to the student, "I appreciate your interest in my well being, but you could have been using this time more constructively for additional Torah study."

It is so tempting to engage in diversion, and it is so easy to rationalize that we need all the diversion. We must be aware of the temptation to idle away precious time. Many people are beyond being seduced by the *yetzer hara* to violate Shabbos or eat non-kosher food. However, they are far more vulnerable to be enticed into excessive diversion. We must recognize that as servants of G-d we are always on full-time duty, and we must not allow ourselves to be diverted from our mission.

Timeless Responsibility

Of the three time frames — past, present, future — we have our best grasp of the present, since we experience it now. We have some grasp of the past, since we have experienced it and it is etched in our memory. The future, however, is an abstraction, and although we speak about it as a reality, we do not relate to it in the same way as we do to the past and present. Small children have no understanding whatever of the future, and tomorrow, next week, or next year are all equally meaningless to them. We improve upon the concept of the future as we mature, but for most of us, it remains a kind of vague concept which does not fully impact on our behavior.

It is evident that our culture lacks a firm awareness of the future. We relentlessly destroy the environment, with systematic elimination of both tropical and temperate forests, abolition of rare species, and pollution of the air and water. The steps that are taken to minimize this destruction are little more than token, as we rationalize our actions, driven by an incessant desire to enrich the present, thereby jeopardizing the future. On an individual basis, intelligent people who are fully aware of the destructive consequences of smoking nevertheless indulge in this most dangerous habit, as if they were immune to its consequences. Both individually and collectively we act as though the future did not exist. We do not wish to deprive ourselves of the pleasures of the present which are real and concrete, for the sake of the future, which is but an abstraction. To deprive ourselves of pleasures in consideration of the future is a kind of *living mesiras nefesh.*

Torah provides a precedent for us. Moses was instructed to designate six cities of refuge for people who have accidentally caused someone death, three in Canaan and three in TransJordan. Although the latter would not become operative until all six were designated, and inasmuch as Moses was to die before the Israelites entered Canaan, there seemed to be little point in his designating the three cities in TransJordan. Nevertheless Moses did so in preparation for the future, a future which he knew he would not live to see.

It is of interest that the verses which tell of Moses' action are immediately followed by the verse, "This is the Torah which Moses set forth before the Children of Israel" (*Deuteronomy* 4:44), a verse which we repeat whenever the Torah is lifted and displayed in shul. Perhaps the message in approximating "This is the Torah" to Moses' action is that the concept of doing whatever you can now and not postponing it for whatever reason is an essential principle of Torah.

Doing things whose results may not be immediately evident is in contrast to a prevailing attitude. I can testify from personal experience that there is relatively little interest in scientific re-search whose results will not be known to the current investigators. Some long-term research does indeed occur, but much valuable information could be gathered if there were more studies which required more than one lifetime. Indeed, I have found relatively little support for a research project whose results would not become known for 10 years. Funding sources are most reluctant to support projects whose results will not be evident within one or two years.

The attitude toward the future may be directly related to one's status of spirituality. As has been pointed out, man is a com-posite creature, with an essentially animal body and a soul which is of Divine origin. The more we emphasize our bodily needs, the more we resemble animals. The more we emphasize our spiritual needs, the more G-dlike we become, as we emu-late the Divine attributes.

Animals do not have an intellectual concept of the future. They may have instinctive behavior which seems to indicate a concept of the future, as when squirrels store away food for the winter, but there is little reason to believe that this an intellectu-al exercise. Animals do not project the consequences of their current actions. Our concept of the future comes from the spir-it, which is of Divine origin, and for whom the future is as real as the present. Thus, the more spiritual we become, the better is our handle on the future, and more responsible our behavior becomes.

One of the Divine attributes is timelessness. Insofar as time is a measurement — minutes, hours, months, years, centuries— and G-d is eternal without any dimensions, time does not apply to G-d, for Whom the past, present, and future are all "present." This is why many of our great *tzaddikim* for whom the body was merely a vehicle to carry out the desires of the *neshamah* as expressed in performance of mitzvos, and who had elevated themselves spiritually, partook of the Divine timelessness and were often able to look into the future.

But even for those who have not reached the dazzling spiritual heights that can lead to prophetic foresight, there can be contemplation of the future. Consideration of the future is certainly not contingent on prophecy, and although such foresight is not infallible, it can guide our actions. Such consideration is a product of the intellect, as the Talmud says, "Who is wise? One who can envision what will come to pass" (*Tamid* 32a).

Our senses can only experience the present, and contemplation of the future is an intellectual activity which may result in our having to deny ourselves the pleasures of the present, which requires a degree of *mesiras nefesh*.

As I have repeatedly pointed out, *mesiras nefesh* is not really a sacrifice. In my clinical work treating people who have become addicted to drugs, I come in contact with people who have ruined their own lives and those of their families because they lived only for the present, and stubbornly refused to contemplate the future. Addiction may be seen as the prototype of neglecting the future in favor of immediate gratification. Someone who gives up smoking in order to save his life is hardly sacrificing anything. Denying oneself pleasures because of contemplation of future consequences is an act of self-preservation rather than one of sacrifice.

Accepting
the Yoke

There are numerous references in Torah literature to the concept of "accepting the yoke." The recitation of the *Shema* is intended to be *kabbalas ol*, acceptance of the yoke of Divine servitude. The most condemning adjective we find in the Torah for an evil person is *ish bliyal*, which means "a person without a yoke," someone devoid of a sense of responsibility.

Accepting the yoke means that one accepts full responsibility for one's actions, and this is a trait which is in rather short supply. Far more often, people seek to place blame on others, and may come to believe their own lies, namely that the fault lies with someone else rather than with themselves. I regret that I must admit that my own profession, psychiatry and psychology, often places blame on a client's parents for his dysfunctional behavior or symptoms. While there is no denying that parents have a major impact on the development of a child's feelings and thoughts, this should not be used as a way of allowing a person to evade responsibility for his own behavior. A much more constructive approach therefore is "Even if you are what your parents made you, if you stay that way it is your own fault."

Living mesiras nefesh requires accepting responsibility and not looking for ways to shirk it. We must be on our guard not to fall prey to rationalizations which exonerate us.

*R*abbi Aryeh Levin of Jerusalem had been a student of the yeshivah of Slutzk, when Rabbi Isser Zalman Melzer had been dean. Many years later, when both resided in Jerusalem, Rabbi Levin would visit his teacher on Friday night. One time Rabbi Isser Zalman asked him where he ate when he was in yeshivah. Some yeshivos did not have dining facilities and dormitories, and the students would have days assigned to local citizens at whose homes they would eat that day's main meal.

Rabbi Levin told him where he ate on Shabbos, and also at whose homes he ate on Sunday, Monday, Tuesday, and Thursday. "What about Wednesday and Friday?" Rabbi Isser Zalman asked. Rabbi Levin reluctantly admitted that he had no place to eat on those two days. "But I remember Wednesdays and Fridays as being the day's on which I studied best."

Much later that night Rabbi Levin heard a knock at the door. It was Rabbi Isser Zalman's wife. "You must come with me," she said. "The Rabbi is beside himself and can find no peace."

Rabbi Levin quickly hurried to his master's home, where he found his teacher pacing the floor and wringing his hands. "I was ignorant of the fact that one of my students had no food two days each week! It was my responsibility to look after your needs and I was derelict. What am I going to say on Judgment Day when they take me into account for my dereliction? Can you forgive me, Reb Aryeh?"

Rabbi Levin tried to reassure his teacher. "There is no need for forgiveness. It was my responsibility to notify the administration. In no way was it your fault." But Rabbi Isser Zalman could not be appeased, and tearfully pleaded with Reb Aryeh to forgive him, which he of course did.

Reb Aryeh was undoubtedly correct. It was his duty to inform the administration of the yeshivah of his needs, and Rabbi Isser Zalman could certainly have had an easy way out of accepting responsibility for the oversight, but he refused to avail himself of it. Rabbi Isser Zalman had a firm grasp on the concept of *kabbalas ol.*

I would like to reiterate the point I made in the Introduction that a living *mesiras nefesh* surpasses that of martyrdom, and that is why G-d responded to Rachel and not to the Patriarchs. Furthermore, it was not Rachel's act of heroism per se that is so important, but rather that she had developed her character to a level of so refined a spiritual perfection that it was easier for her to accept a lifetime deprived of the man she had been prepared to marry rather than to see her sister publicly humiliated, even if that humiliation lasted only for a brief moment.

One might ask: In what way did Rachel surpass the Patriarch Abraham? His act of *mesiras nefesh* would have sentenced him to the deprivation of his beloved son for the rest of his life. This seems to prove his *mesiras nefesh* was at least equal to that of Rachel. The answer is that while Abraham was indeed ready to sacrifice the remainder of his days, this was following a direct commandment by G-d. Rachel had no such Divine revelation that told her to reveal the secret password to her sister. It was rather by her own efforts that she had elevated herself to a status where another person's dignity took precedence over her most intense emotions.

This is the kind of greatness that Rabbi Isser Zalman demonstrated. He had developed a sense of responsibility so great that he held himself culpable for something which really was not an oversight, since the initiative should have been taken by the student. The kind of sensitivity that Rachel had about allowing another person to be humiliated, and the kind of sensitivity that a dean of a yeshivah felt for his students, is the substance that comprises *living mesiras nefesh*.

Because the concept of responsibility is so crucial to Torah life, I must digress here to point out how misleading some secular concepts may be. Torah divides a person's life into two phases: *katan*, or minor, and *gadol*, adult. A minor is not legally responsible for his actions, and this responsibility falls upon his parents' shoulders. This prevails until one becomes *bar-* or *bas-mitzvah*, 13 for a boy, 12 for a girl. When the *bar-mitzvah* is called to the Torah for the first time, the father makes a public declaration of gratitude to G-d "for removing the burden of punishment of this child from me," because at nightfall of the 12th or 11th year, a sudden transformation occurs, and the child becomes an adult. The boy of 13 and the girl of 12 are full-fledged adults, who are as responsible for their actions as a man or woman of 40. It is important to take note: There is no hiatus of responsibility. At any given time someone is fully responsible for the youngster's actions: the father when the child is a minor, and the youngster when he/she becomes of age.

Western civilization introduced a new concept: *adolescence*, and I can tell you from clinical experience that many parents silently berate whoever thought up this concept. Adolescence is a period of no man's land. The youngster is not held responsible for his actions because he is not yet an adult, and the parents cannot be held responsible because he has grown up beyond their control. A new system of adjudication was developed, of "juvenile law and juvenile courts," which is a chaotic situation, because there seems to be nothing one can do with these "juveniles." They cannot be released without proper discipline because they are a threat to society; at the same time they cannot be properly disciplined because they are only "juveniles." The epidemic of adolescent drug use and adolescent crime which is sweeping the country is no doubt one of the consequences of this absurd concoction of "adolescence," a secular concept which has no place in Torah and *halachah*.

But let me take this one step further. Once the genie is out of the bottle you can never put him back. Once a youngster has experienced a period of several years of diminished responsibility, he may never acquire a full sense of responsibility, even when he reaches the age of legal majority. To make matters worse, even the latter is hopelessly confused, because the age of legal majority varies from state to state, and even within one state there are different stages for majority: one for driving an automobile, another for service in the army, another for smoking, another for drinking, another for marriage, and yet another for voting. This chaotic situation is the result of "sophisticated" secularism, whereas the "primitive" Torah made it abundantly clear: Majority occurs at the moment *bar-* or *bas-mitzvah* age is reached, and is upheld across the board.

I have elaborated on this concept because of the pivotal nature of *kabbalas ol*, assumption of responsibility in Torah. Unfortunately, living in an environment where we cannot implement *halachah* via the Torah judicial system, our children are subjected to the misguided cultural concept of "adolescence." To combat this we must emphasize the importance of responsibility in our own lives, to serve as models for our children. When we make a mistake, we should admit it and accept the consequences. Too often we try to defend our mistakes and justify our misdeeds, but absolving ourselves from responsibility sets a bad example for our children. Admitting our mistakes and taking the consequences may require a *mesiras nefesh*, but as with other types of *mesiras nefesh,* this is hardly a sacrifice. If, by being role models for *kabbalas ol* we succeed in teaching our children to accept responsibility, this is a reward that far outweighs any of the inconveniences that might accrue from fully accepting responsibility for our actions.

When Fear Is Healthy

We often hear the term *yiras shamayim*, the fear of Heaven, and we generally interpret this to mean that a person should fear G-d. The *mussar* writings state that the concept is not that one should live in fear of being punished for sin, but rather that one should have so great a feeling of awe and reverence for G-d that to transgress His will is unthinkable.

There is yet another interpretation of *yiras shamayim*, and that is that one should have the same fear as does G-d. Although G-d is in control of everything in the universe, He has divested Himself of the control of people's moral behavior. As the Talmud puts it, "Everything is in the hands of G-d except the reverence of G-d" (*Berachos* 33b).

A person is totally free to choose between right and wrong, and G-d does not intervene to prevent a person from committing a morally improper act. Yet, G-d wishes us to do right, and it grieves Him when we do wrong. It is therefore much the same situation as a parent watching his child from afar and seeing him standing perilously close to the curb. He is afraid that the child may run into the street, but is helpless to do anything about it. Similarly, since G-d does not intervene in our moral behavior, He is, as it were, by His own choice powerless to stop a person from doing wrong; hence He is fearful that we may do so and harm ourselves. Thus, G-d does have a fear: the fear that a person will sin, and that is *yiras shamayim*, the fear had by G-d.

We, too, should be fearful of doing wrong because it will harm us. We should thus have *yiras shamayim*, and share in the Divine fear. If the conviction that deviating from G-d's will is detrimental to our own welfare will stimulate our innate drive for self-preservation, this fear will be to our own advantage.

We cannot fathom the Divine wisdom, and must accept as axioms the principles that our Torah luminaries have postulated, namely, that G-d put man on earth, to live in conditions which are conducive to gratifying one's physical drives, and to resist these drives when they are contrary to the Divine rules for human behavior. Surrounded by countless temptations, we are at any one moment at risk of succumbing to temptation. Furthermore, we have within us a cunning and powerful *yetzer hara*, which can distort our thought processes and judgment so that we may see wrong as right. Under such circumstances, it is only natural that we maintain a *yiras shamayim*, a fear that we may err. We must also realize that our behavior is subject to a law of nature that "mitzvah begets mitzvah and sin begets sin," and that any improper act, even if committed inadvertently, renders us more vulnerable to other misdeeds.

It might appear that maintaining an attitude of fear may cause some discomfort, and if this is so, we must accept this with *mesiras nefesh*, setting aside the quest for comfort in order to live properly according to Torah values. But this may not even be so. There is a difference between *anxiety*, which is a destructive emotion, and *healthy fear*, which is constructive.

The Talmud relates that Rabbi Yishmael noticed that one of his students was anxious, and he said, "You must have done something wrong that causes you to feel this way." The student responded, "Why? Is it not written, 'Happy is the person who is always in fear'?" Rabbi Yishmael said, "No, that does not refer to anxiety. That refers to fear of transgressing Torah" (Berachos 60a).

Here the Talmud makes a clear distinction between anxiety, which is an indication that something has gone awry within a person, and fear of wrongdoing, which is a healthy feeling that protects us from behaving improperly.

We can now see that there is room for two opposite feelings: *bitachon*, security, and *yirah*, fear. We should feel secure in those areas that are controlled by G-d, which includes everything except our moral and ethical behavior. The latter, which G-d does not control, and in which we are left to our own resources, is where we should have fear. Too often the situation is reversed, with people being very anxious about their financial situation, but feeling very content and safe in the spiritual sphere. Achieving a proper perspective, to feel content with whatever we have materially and to be uneasy about our spiritual life, requires an attitude of *mesiras nefesh*.

Seeing Is Not Believing

Every reasonable person accepts the validity of the age-old idiom "Seeing is believing." It would seem irrational to deny the evidence of one's senses.

The philosopher, Descartes, called attention to the fact that sense impressions are not invariably correct. He points out that a person who is hallucinating may see something very vividly, even though the object does not exist in reality. I have abundant experiences in my clinical practice of people who are certain of what they hear and what they see, although neither the sounds nor the visual impressions are true. Strangely enough, people who hallucinate voices are more certain of the reality of the sound than normal people who hear a spoken voice.

But let us leave philosophical discussions and clinical examples aside and get down to everyday life experiences. We do not assume that we are hallucinating, and we do adjust to reality according to what we see and hear. However, it is one thing to see and hear, and another thing to interpret *what* we see and hear. Sometimes the obvious interpretations of our sense impressions may be misleading. It is simple to allow ourselves to coast along with obvious impressions, and it may take effort to overcome these impressions and come to different conclusions.

The Rabbi of Kotzk cites the tragic episode of the spies sent by Moses to scout Canaan, whose pessimistic report sealed the doom of an entire generation, and cast a pall upon Jewish history from which we have not emerged thousands of years later. He asked: Why was G-d's wrath so severe? After all, the spies told the truth about what they had seen: fortified cities, a race of giants, mighty warriors. Why were they so severely punished for reporting the truth?

The Rabbi answers that it was the interpretation of their sense perceptions that was wrong. G-d had promised that the Israelites would conquer the land, and G-d's word was not to be doubted. Reality, said the Rabbi of Kotzk, is not what you think it to be, but what G-d says it is.

The chassidic master, Rabbi Baruch of Mezhibozh, was once reciting the prayer before Kiddush Friday night, and when he came to the phrase, "I thank You, G-d, for all the kindnesses You have done with me and for all the kindnesses that You will do with me in the future," he paused. "Why should I thank G-d in advance for future kindnesses? I can thank Him for those kindnesses when they transpire." After a few moments' thought he said, "Ah! I understand. It is possible that when these kindnesses occur, I will not recognize them as such. In fact, I may think them to be adversities, and I will not be aware that I must be thankful to G-d. That is why I must do so in ad-

vance." Then Rabbi Baruch began to weep. "How tragic it is that we can be so unperceptive. Just think of it! G-d will be doing kindnesses with me, and I may be unable to appreciate them as such."

There are many times when we may feel distressed by unpleasant happenings in our lives. Turning over one's senses and one's apprehensions to G-d is not easy, and is a kind of *mesiras nefesh.*

The Chafetz Chaim states that in the Biblical epic of Joseph and his brothers, the latter must have been totally bewildered by the series of strange events that were happening to them. Why were they being unjustly accused of being spies? Why was the viceroy insistent on their bringing their youngest brother to Egypt? How did the viceroy know their ages and which of them were full brothers and which were half brothers? When Joseph revealed his identity to them and said, "I am Joseph," these few words explained everything. There was no need for any further elaboration. All that had previously been inexplicable had now become perfectly clear.

Similarly, said the Chafetz Chaim, we cannot understand what has happened to us throughout our history, but when the Redemption occurs and G-d reveals Himself to us and says, "I am your G-d," we will understand everything with perfect clarity.

Until the time of the Redemption, one who has a firm conviction that G-d is in control of the world and that His benevolence is unlimited can have the concept that everything is with a purpose, and everything fits in with the Divine master plan. It does take a *living mesiras nefesh* to set aside our own perceptions and conclude that what we believe is more true than what we see.

Occasionally we are privileged to recognize *hashgachah pratis*, Divine providence, at work. We can all recall incidents which we considered to be mishaps at the time they occurred, only to discover at some later date that these were really blessings in disguise. But in spite of such observations, when something unpleasant occurs, we again agonize over the misfortune. It takes a constant presence of mind and reinforcement to maintain our belief in Divine benevolence. Incidentally, *emunah* or belief is not the same as credulousness, which is the belief of simpletons (*Proverbs* 14:16). *Emunah* is constantly subject to challenges, and we must find ways to strengthen our *emunah*. Little wonder that it is recommended that we recite *Ani maamin,* the 13 principles of faith each day.

Chassidic lore has many accounts of *tzaddikim* who were asked by their *chassidim* for a specific *berachah*, which they refused to give. They explained that the *chassid* was asking for something which he thought was to his advantage, but the *tzaddik* understood that fulfillment of this particular wish would be detrimental to him. Indeed, in our prayers for the new month we pray that G-d fulfill all the desires of our hearts *that are for our good,* which indicates an awareness that not everything we desire and pray for is necessarily beneficial for us.

We generally associate the *mesiras nefesh* of the *Shema* with martyrdom. Countless Jews who surrendered their lives for *kiddush Hashem* died with the words of the *Shema* on their lips, declaring their unwavering faith in *Hashem*. But we have been discussing *living mesiras nefesh,* and the *Shema* can apply to this as readily as to martyrdom.

It is customary to cover our eyes when we recite the *Shema.* My father offered the following explanation for this practice.

In the *Shema* we refer to G-d in two ways (1) *Hashem,* the Ineffable Name, and (2) *Elokenu.* These two appellations refer to two manifestations of Divine management of the world. When we can see the Divine mercy, kindness, and compassion, we refer to G-d as *Hashem.* When it appears to us that G-d is exercising firmness and harsh judgment, we refer to Him as *Elokenu.* We believe, however, that nothing bad ever emanates from G-d (*Lamentations* 3:38), and even though we may consider something to be a harsh judgment, characterized by

Elokenu, the truth of the matter is that it is really a kindness which bears an external cloak of harshness; i.e., there is in fact only one way in which *Hashem* conducts the world, and that is with *chessed* (kindness). Sometimes this is readily apparent, and at other times it is concealed.

This principle is a matter of belief, because our human perception sees adversities as being harsh. To indicate that our belief overrides our perception, we cover our eyes as we say that *Hashem* and *Elokenu* are *echad*, one and the same. Subordinating our sensory perceptions to our convictions is an act of *mesiras nefesh*, hence the *Shema* is as relevant to *living mesiras nefesh* as it is to martyrdom.

We often think of the *Shema* as the last words of our martyrs who paid the ultimate price repudiating *avodah zarah* (idolatry), and declaring their unfaltering faith in *Hashem*. We may also think that *avodah zarah* is something of a historical nature, and that in modern-day life there is no reason for concern about *avodah zarah*. In an important essay, Rabbi Yerucham Levovitz points out that this is a serious error (*Da'as Chochmah Umussar*, vol. 4, 291-297).

Rabbi Yerucham calls attention to the prophet's lengthy admonition against *avodah zarah*, instructing people to distinguish between the true G-d, Creator of the universe, and the false gods of idolatry (*Jeremiah* 10), and he asks what need was there for such distinction. Doesn't every sensible person know that a statue fashioned by human hands is nothing but a lifeless, powerless dummy?

Rabbi Yerucham explains that in order for there to be *bechirah* (free choice), G-d created forces of evil that do have powers that are commensurate with those of *kedushah* and the forces of good. These evil forces have the capacity of deluding people and of presenting them with false sense experiences, even with hallucinations that appear more real than reality. He cites the *Midrash* that when Moses failed to return from Sinai when the Israelites expected him, Satan conjured up a scene where angels were carrying the deceased Moses on a bier, and the Israelites saw with their own eyes that Moses had died. In their confusion and depression, they were vulnerable to commit the sin of the golden calf.

This capacity to delude people did not evaporate with the decline of paganism. We may not be attracted to idol worship, but we are still prone to be taken in by delusional thinking. This aspect of *avodah zarah* still exists, strong as ever.

Moses repeatedly alerted us to this. He pointed out that there may be false prophets who perform seemingly supernatural feats and use them as evidence of their authenticity, and he warns us not to be misled by their claims, because G-d has given these false prophets the ability to perform miraculous deeds to test our faith in Him (*Deuteronomy* 13:2-6). At an even more practical level, Moses warns us not to think that our successes are due to our own cunning and efforts, and to realize that everything we have is a Divine gift (ibid. 8:11-18). Failure to ascribe everything to *Hashem* is essentially *avodah zarah*.

Rabbi Schneur Zalman in *Tanya* elaborates on this theme, and states that it is a mistake to even think that anything that transpires is a result of a combination of *Hashem*'s blessing *together with* a natural force, whether it be a physical law of nature or the forces of the market place. There is nothing that *combines* with *Hashem*, and it is purely and solely *Hashem* that brings anything and everything about. True, we must make an effort at earning a livelihood because so it was decreed upon Adam, but we are essentially just going through the motions. What we achieve or fail to achieve is not cause and effect of our own efforts.

Consider this scenario. You happen to hear about a piece of property that is available, and your research leads you to believe that this property will increase significantly in value. You buy the property, and after a short period of time you happily discover that you were right, and that a developer is willing to buy this property from you at a huge profit for you. How shrewd you were!

You may be shocked to hear that you have fallen into the trap of *avodah zarah!* You, who are so meticulous about observing *glatt kosher* and not missing a single day of *davening*, are actually guilty of one of the cardinal sins. It seems absurd!

It may seem absurd, Rabbi Yerucham says, but not to realize that it was *Hashem* who put the idea of the purchase in your mind is nothing less than *avodah zara*. Onkeles interprets the verse in *Deuteronomy* 8:18 to read that "it is G-d Who gives you the idea to acquire properties." How much more explicit can one get?

To deny that which appears to us to be obvious takes *mesiras nefesh*. Yes, when we recite the *Shema* we cover our eyes, because much of what we see and think can be hallucinatory and delusional, and when we say the *Shema*, we must repudiate all kinds of *avodah zarah,* which is not restricted to pagan worship of idols.

In Search of Tranquility

f we are to judge by the many millions of prescriptions written by physicians for various tranquilizing medications, and add to these the number of over-the-counter drugs and the amount of alcohol consumed, and then add the myriad of relaxation books, tapes and devices purchased, we can come to only one conclusion: The most overwhelming human drive is for tranquility. In modern times, stress has become a no-no, something to be avoided at all costs. While it is true that there are kinds of stress that are either quantitatively or qualitatively injurious, the fact is that many people seek to escape not only from the latter, but from all kinds of stress. Unfortunately, many purveyors of health services comply with this request, so that we are now the most medicated and "therapized" society in world history.

But just what is wrong with this? Why refer to tranquility in so critical a tone, as if it were something sinful? It is hardly a crime to wish to be at peace.

This is another example of the difference between Torah values and secular values, and it is an indication of how we may be carried away with the tide, incorporating concepts which are antithetical to Torah without being aware of it.

There is a *Midrash,* quoted by Rashi in *Genesis* 37:1. The Patriarch Jacob, having survived persecution by his brother Esau, and having been ruthlessly exploited by his wicked father-in-law, Laban, finally returned to the ancestral home at the age of 95, and wished to settle and live in peace. But G-d decided otherwise. "Is it not enough for *tzaddikim* that they are destined to enjoy bliss in the Eternal World, that they seek to be tranquil on earth as well? This shall not be!" Whereupon Jacob was then subjected to 22 years of torment, grieving over the loss of his beloved son, Joseph, whom he assumed to have been killed.

The obvious question is raised by numerous commentaries. Just what was wrong with the Patriarch's wish to enjoy some peace of mind? We know that Jacob was a highly spiritual person who spent all his time in the study of Torah as it had been transmitted by Abraham and Isaac, and as he had learned it from Shem and Eber. Certainly if he had been at peace, he would have continued his spiritual pursuits. Why was he taken to task for seeking tranquility?

Rabbi Yerucham Levovitz states that this *Midrash* teaches us that this earthly world was created for people to struggle in so that they might perfect themselves, as the Scripture states "for man was born to struggle" (*Job* 5:7). Being tranquil defeats the purpose. A person might think that the ideal situation for study of Torah and performance of . is to be free of all other distractions and responsibilities, and thus be free to devote oneself totally to spiritual pursuits. This is a grave error, says Rabbi Yerucham. It is precisely under the burdens of stress that we can achieve proper Torah study and performance of mitzvos.

This theme is echoed in Torah literature. The *Zohar* states that the spies sent by Moses discouraged the Israelites from the conquest of Canaan because they believed that if they remained in the desert, sustained by the miraculous manna from heaven and the well of Miriam, protected by the clouds of glory and without need to provide for themselves, they could totally devote themselves to Torah study, whereas if they entered Canaan, the miracles would end, and they would be diverted by the need to work the fields and engage in commerce. Their fatal mistake was that it was G-d's wish that they live a normal life and while coping with the stresses of everyday life, study Torah and fulfill the mitzvos.

We find this again in *Ethics of the Fathers* (6:4), "This is the way of Torah: Eat bread with salt, drink water by the measure, and sleep on the earth." And, "Torah has no staying power unless one is ready to sacrifice himself for it" (*Shabbos* 83b). It is thus evident that serious Torah study and comfort are antithetical.

I once asked a noted Torah educator why it was that with the vast proliferation of full-time Torah students in this country, who sincerely dedicate themselves to Torah study, that we have not produced a single Reb Moshe. We indeed have many fine Torah scholars, and there are some with extraordinary intellectual capacities and excellent memories, yet we do not have anyone who approaches Reb Moshe. His answer was, "You don't produce a Reb Moshe with Pepsi-Cola." Reb Moshe's daily diet as a student was dark bread and radish, and there were days when even that was lacking. Our Torah students are much more fortunate, and even though they may not live in luxury, they generally do not experience grave material deprivation, and it seems that it is precisely the latter that is the catalyst for Torah excellence.

We know all this because we learned it from G-d's response to the Patriarch Jacob and from the Talmudic sources, but the Patriarch had no way of knowing this, and it was his understanding that having a clear, unburdened mind would be most conducive to Torah study, hence his aspiration for tranquility.

Furthermore, tranquility is very close to contentment, and being content with oneself is certainly not compatible with sincere *avodas Hashem*, Divine worship.

This is the message in the well-known anecdote of Rav Saadya Gaon, who once lodged at an inn, but the innkeeper was unaware of the identity of his illustrious guest. When he found out that he had hosted Rav Saadya Gaon, he apologized to the great sage for not having accorded him proper respect. The sage replied, "You have nothing to apologize for. You treated me admirably," whereupon the innkeeper said, "But if I had only known who you were, I would have treated you with even greater respect." Rav Saadya Gaon began to weep. "Yesterday I worshipped G-d according to my grasp of His greatness then. If only I knew yesterday what I know today, my worship would have been of a much higher quality."

We should never be content with our spiritual achievement. To the contrary, every advance in spirituality should make us more humble, as we should stand in greater awe and with increasing reverence for the Infinite.

Rabbi Isser Zalman Meltzer used to tell the following story about Rabbi Hillel of Horodna, who was the son-in-law of Rabbi Chaim of Volozhin.

One of the chassidic masters visited Horodna, and Rabbi Hillel heard that people consulted the Rebbe for ways to improve their level of yiras shamayim, reverence for G-d. As this was in the period when chassidism was looked at with suspicion and the relationship between chassidim and Rabbi Hillel's congregation was quite strained, Rabbi Hillel was hesitant to consult the

Rebbe. However, his feelings that he was derelict in yiras shamayim overcame his misgivings, and he decided to visit the Rebbe and not disclose his identity.

When Rabbi Hillel met the Rebbe, he said, "I have heard that the Rebbe gives helpful advice how to improve one's yiras shamayim. I am not content with my yiras shamayim, and I would like the Rebbe to give me some advice how I can improve myself."

The Rebbe responded, "I have no standard guidelines. If someone tells me something about himself, what his life-style is like, perhaps I can give him some helpful suggestions."

Rabbi Hillel felt himself trapped, because now he would have to reveal much about himself, and perhaps even disclose his identity. But there was no way out.

"As you can see," Rabbi Hillel said to the Rebbe, "I am well along in years, and I am no longer engaged in business. People at my age do not sleep long, so I arise early in the morning. What can I do so early in the morning? I go to shul and learn until the time for prayer, then I daven (pray). Sometimes people ask if they can learn together with me, so I end up teaching some Mishnah and perhaps Gemara (Talmud). After davening I have breakfast, and since I am idle, I learn until lunch, then rest a bit. Sometimes people come to consult me with their personal or business problems. They think that because I am old I have acquired enough experience to help them solve their problems. This goes on until Minchah time, when I go to shul, and again some people ask to learn with me. After Maariv and supper, I either learn alone or with some people. That is how my day goes, and as I said, I am not content with my level of yiras shamayim."

The Rebbe smiled and said, "As I see, you daven, study Torah, teach Torah, and assist in communal problems. Woe unto you, Rabbi Hillel, Rabbi of Horodna, if you would be content with your level of yiras shamayim!"

Rabbi Isser Zalman would tell this story and point out that it is precisely one's intense devotion to Torah and mitzvos that should make him dissatisfied with his level of *yiras shamayim* and stimulate him to even further spiritual growth.

We learn from the *Midrash* about the Patriarch Jacob that we are not to aspire to tranquility. However, while tranquility is not desirable, serenity is to be sought, and there is a substantial difference between the two. Tranquility is the absence of stress and discomfort, while serenity is accepting stress and discomfort and not being rendered dysfunctional by them. This is what is meant when the Talmud (*Berachos* 60b) says that a person is to make a *berachah* (blessing) of gratitude to G-d for everything that transpires, whether it is good or bad, and that one must do so with *simchah*. Rashi makes a point of translating *simchah* in this context not as "joy" but as "with complete trust." Rashi clearly means that it is unrealistic to expect the average person to be joyous in the face of adversity, but one should be able to develop the trust in G-d that everything that happens is for an ultimate good, and one should not be shattered when things do not go well.

This too is something we learn from the Patriarch Jacob, whose desire for tranquility was countered to by his suffering resulting from the disappearance of Joseph. The *Midrash* states that Jacob complained, "G-d has turned away from me," whereupon G-d said, "I am manipulating things to make his son viceroy of the mightiest empire in the world, and he complains that I am turning away from him!" The saga of Joseph is to teach us that while we may not be able to see the good in adversity, we should have trust in G-d that He is not neglecting us, and this constitutes serenity.

As mentioned, some people in search of tranquility may seek it in the numbing effects of alcohol. For an alcoholic to recover, he must aim for serenity rather than tranquility. Life is never without stress, and giving up the tranquilizing chemical will bring one face to face with life's hardships, and one must learn how to cope with them. As one recovering person aptly put it, "I was told that if I stopped drinking, things would get better. That was not true. Things did not get better. Rather, I got better."

The "*guf*" desires tranquility, freedom from discomfort. Making serenity the desired aim requires surrendering this "*guf*" aspiration, in what we strangely enough term *mesiras nefesh*.

Each Penny Counts

We are all honest people. In no way would we knowingly cheat or take away another person's belongings. But this hardly requires *mesiras nefesh*.

However, there are things that we may do inadvertently that we would not think of as being improper. Yet, the laws of the Torah are extremely exacting, and true observance of all the laws that pertain to property rights may indeed require a *living mesiras nefesh*.

The Talmud states that respect for another's property is so basic that it can be found in nature, and that even if the Torah had not been given to us, we would have been accountable in that we should have learned this ethic by observing the lowly ant. Solomon says, "You indolent person, go to the ant, see its ways and become wise" (*Proverbs* 6:6), upon which the *Midrash* comments that if an ant has secured a particle of food and leaves it, no other ant will touch it (*Devarim Rabbah* 5:2)

The Talmud is unusually harsh in its condemnation of one who takes what is not his, for whereas giving *tzedakah* can merit forgiveness for various transgressions, it does not do so for unjust possession. "A person has two hands. If he steals with one and gives *tzedakah* with the other, he will not be cleansed in the Eternal World" (*Midrash Mishlei* 11).

How serious this transgression is can be seen from the behavior of our great Torah personalities. The Chafetz Chaim never allowed a single moment to be wasted, and was scrupulous in accounting for every second. Yet, when he distributed his books, he laboriously leafed through each one lest there be a page missing, and the purchaser perchance receive a defective product. Think of the hours he spent doing this, because he considered this to take precedence even over his precious study of Torah!

Some people might consider such scrupulosity to be fanaticism, but our giants of Torah were people who deliberated on every move, and did not behave irrationally. They were as meticulous about every cent in their possession as with every other Torah requirement.

Rabbi Eliahu Dushnitzer was the *mashgiach* (dean of students) of the Lomza yeshivah. He was extremely frugal with the use of electricity, because the yeshivah paid his electric bill. He would extinguish the lights and study by the glow of a kerosene lamp, explaining, "I occasionally doze off in the midst of my learning, and it is unfair to the yeshivah that they pay for the lights burning while I sleep."

I have often observed people at the check-out counter returning excessive change that was erroneously given to them. There is no question that they do not wish to enrich themselves in the least at someone else's expense. However, the anecdotes about our Torah personalities show us that there may be minor infringements on other's property rights that may escape our attention.

I was privileged to have personal contact with the Steipler Gaon, whose brilliant commentaries on the Talmud have made his *sefarim* (books) extremely well received. His caution not to profit unjustly from his books was beyond the most taxing ethical principles. For example, if a yeshivah student wished to purchase several of his volumes, he would ask him what tractate of Talmud he was studying at the time, and would sell him only the volume of his works that was relevant to that tractate. The Steipler's eyesight was poor, and he could not see how much money people had left in payment for his books. Since people often wished to give the *tzaddik* a gift, they would leave money over and above the price of the books. When the Steipler would discover this, he would be in anguish, and did not rest until the excess money was returned.

A shochet (ritual slaughterer) came to Rabbi Yisrael of Salant and told him that he wished to give up being a shochet, and open a store for his livelihood. "I cannot live with the awesome responsibilities of being a shochet," he said. "If I err in the performance of my work, I may cause people to eat treifah." Rabbi Yisrael said, "Treifah is indeed a serious sin. But do you realize how many pitfalls of sin there are in doing business? '(1) You shall not steal;(2) You shall not rob;(3) You shall not covet; (4) You shall not deceive;(5) You shall not lie;(6) You shall not withhold wages;(7) You shall not have inaccurate weights and measures.' If your conscience torments you about inadvertently doing wrong as a shochet, how much more should it bother you in transacting business!"

There is yet another important teaching that flows from a sincere commitment against wrongful possession. Although vidui (confession) is an essential component of teshuvah and applies to all sins, it is noteworthy that the Torah introduces the concept of vidui in regard to one who does teshuvah for stealing. Why was this particular sin chosen as the focus of *vidui?*

All human faculties derive from G-d, and they were given to man to enable him to carry out the Divine will by behaving properly. These faculties were "loaned" to man for the duration of his sojourn on earth.

If a person lends an object to someone and specifies how it is to be used, *halachah* states that it may not be used for any other purpose. If a person lends someone his automobile with the restriction that it be driven only over level terrain, then the borrower is not permitted to drive it over hills. If he does, it is equivalent to stealing, since he is using another person's possession without the owner's permission.

Inasmuch as G-d gave us our faculties to be used exclusively in His service, using them for any other purpose is in violation of the conditions of the loan, and this is equivalent to stealing. From this perspective, every transgression is a misuse of the faculties loaned to us by G-d, hence *teshuvah* for any sin requires a *vidui* for theft.

Recognizing that all our faculties are merely on loan to us and we are restricted in their use indeed requires a degree of *mesiras nefesh*.

To Know Oneself

In virtually all of my writings, I have stressed the importance of attaining a true self-knowledge, which will invariably result in self-esteem and self-confidence. I have indicated that many people labor under delusions of inadequacy, inferiority, and unworthiness, and I have pointed out that an accurate self-knowledge and a healthy self-esteem are essential for optimum functioning and performance of Torah and mitzvos. I have tried to clarify that feelings of inferiority which stem from a faulty self-perception do not constitute *anivus* (humility), and have cited the pungent words of the ethicist Rabbi Leib Chasman, who said, "A person who is not aware of his talents and strengths is not humble, but rather a fool."

One might think that ridding oneself of inferiority would provide so great a sense of relief that everyone would welcome it.

The fact, however, is otherwise. In my clinical experience I have seen people hang on tenaciously to these negative feelings, and when their true worth is pointed out to them, they find ways to discount this evidence. One can only come to the conclusion that there is some psychological gain in feeling inadequate!

It is not too difficult to explain this apparently irrational phenomenon. *Awareness of one's capacities places a responsibility upon a person to live up to these capacities.* A person who knows that he has the ability to learn will feel guilty if he is derelict in learning. A person who knows that he has the capacity to perform and produce will feel guilty if he does not do so. His option is to either overcome his inertia and do what he is capable of doing, or yield to his indolent inclinations. Inasmuch as the latter will generate guilt, he may convince himself that he really lacks the capacity to be productive, so that he can be more comfortable when doing nothing.

One young man was admitted to my facility for treatment of alcoholism. He came grudgingly, coerced by his parents, and denying that he had a drinking problem. Once admitted, he began asking for various tests to detect whether he had sustained brain damage from his drinking, and whereas he had previously minimized how much he drank, he now exaggerated. He simply could not be reassured that he did not have brain damage. Puzzled by his obsession with this, I had a long therapy session with him, during which it became evident that he was hoping we would find that he indeed did have brain damage! But why would anyone want to have so horrible a diagnosis? Because this would give him a perfect excuse and exonerate him from all responsibilities. He would then be able to say to his parents, "You can't expect me to stay sober. I don't have the ability to do that. Don't you understand? I'm brain damaged! You can't expect me to go to school or hold a job. I'm brain damaged!" The desire to be left alone

*and allowed to drink was so strong that he was willing to
be considered brain damaged to achieve it.*

While this is indeed an extreme example, it is by no means
an isolated occurrence. Many young people give up on themselves and fail to study because they think they cannot grasp
the material.

It is nothing less than amazing how little we appreciate our
capacities. Rabbi Chaim Shmulevitz cites the Talmud which
states that the prophet Samuel's mother, who was barren,
prayed for a child who would be average in every way, "Not too
bright and not too dull." When she brought the young Samuel
to the High Priest, Eli, she said, "*This* is the child I prayed for,"
which means that her prayers were answered to the letter, and
that Samuel was just an average child. "Just think of it!" Rabbi
Shmulevitz said. "Samuel, who the Talmud states was as great
as Moses and Aaron combined, was a person of only average
talents." How dare any person resign himself to mediocre
achievements on the assumption that he is not qualified to do
better?

The *yetzer hara* has a vast arsenal of tactics to prevent a person from fulfilling his mission on earth. Some people can be
enticed to openly violate the Torah. There are those who the
yetzer hara knows cannot be seduced to eat a cheeseburger or
violate Shabbos. With these it may use the tactic of "Why extend yourself to study Torah? You don't have the brains for it.
Don't try the impossible" "Why try to advance yourself? You will
only fail, then you will be worse off with a disappointment. Just
leave well enough alone." In this way the *yetzer hara* crushes a
person, who then fails to assert himself in many constructive
ways. A person should therefore recognize self-denigrating
thoughts as being the work of the *yetzer hara*, and resist succumbing to them.

In *Life's Too Short* (St. Martin's Press 1995) I presented a
variety of symptoms that emanate from a faulty, negative self-

concept, and suggested ways of enhancing one's self-esteem. As mentioned, such an awareness will upset the complacency of resignation to a lesser level of achievement, and this is why gaining a true self-awareness is a component of *living mesiras nefesh*. We will see how this applies to the topic of the next chapter.

To Always Rejoice

Earlier we eluded to living on "manual" rather than on "automatic," and that doing so requires a *living mesiras nefesh*. Nowhere is this as evident as in maintaining an attitude of *simchah* (joy).

We generally assume that our emotions are not under voluntary control, and that our moods are determined by the circumstances we live under at any given time. Thus, if one has good heath, adequate finances, a happy marriage, children who are well, wonderful friends, etc., then one will be in a cheerful mood. Conversely, if one is unhealthy, suffers pain, is in dire economic straits, and has a poor family relationship, one will be despondent. The Talmud states that this is not necessarily so, and "*tzaddikim* have voluntary control of their emotions" (*Bereshis Rabbah* 34:11). This Talmudic statement is not in keeping with conventional wisdom, which assumes that we are not in control of our moods. This is a clear distinction between the secular approach, which assumes that with the exception of those things that require deliberation, people operate on automatic, and the Torah approach, that requires us to operate on manual.

It is a mitzvah in the Torah to be joyous (*Deuteronomy* 15:16), and the Torah even predicts harsh consequences for one who fails to serve G-d with *simchah* (ibid. 28:47). If *simchah* were a spontaneous emotion, beyond voluntary control, the Torah would not have commanded us to do something beyond our capacity. Clearly we are capable of generating *simchah*.

There is a mitzvah of tithing from the produce of one's farms, and after one has delivered all the tithes to the appropriate recipients, there is a declaration one must make, wherein one states, "I have hearkened to the words of my G-d, and I have done all that You have commanded me" (*Deuteronomy* 26:12-15). On the latter verse, Rashi comments, "I rejoiced and I gave joy to others." One of the commentaries remarks, "How is it possible for a person to say that he has fully obeyed the word of G-d, and has fulfilled *all* the Divine commandments? Such a statement appears both presumptuous and vain." He answers, "This is why Rashi adds an explanatory comment. If a person has indeed rejoiced in performing the mitzvah of helping the needy by tithing, and if he has brought joy to them, then he has indeed fulfilled the requirements of Torah. Rabbi Akiva stated that "Love your neighbor as yourself" is the all-encompassing principle of Torah, and if a person cares for others and takes pleasure in doing so, he may truthfully state that he has done all that G-d asks of him.

The Chafetz Chaim points out that a true Torah orientation will result in simchah. "Just imagine," the Chafetz

Chaim says, "that a person was called to the palace for an audience with the king, and that furthermore, the king showed him great affection and assigned him to an important mission. How honored this person would feel! He would certainly tell all his friends about his good fortune, and his joy would be so great that he would forget about his aches and pains and every other thing that had been bothering him.

"If this is so with a mortal king, how much more so should a person be ecstatic with joy that the Sovereign of the Universe invites him to an audience daily, chooses him for a mission, and promises him a great reward upon its completion. Surely this person could not contain his feelings, and would dance with joy.

"If we are not in a state of sublime happiness," says the Chafetz Chaim, "it is because we are lacking in conviction as to our relationship with G-d, and this is a dereliction in emunah (faith)."

Some people may argue that the *mussar* (ethical) writings, by taking us to task for our character defects and transgressions, tend to depress us. Furthermore, if one is to do *teshuvah* and be in a constant state of remorse because of one's sins, this precludes having an upbeat attitude.

This is by no means correct. The Baal Shem Tov was once told of a chazzan (cantor) who had the unusual practice of chanting the al chet (confession of sins) with a lively melody instead of the traditional somber tone. The chazzan explained, "Suppose I had the job as janitor in the palace, and I was engaged in cleaning up the palace, riding it of all dirt, and beautifying it for the king. Would I not be happy that I had the good fortune to do this? When I confess my sins, I rid myself of material that is objectionable to G-d, and I make myself into a more hospitable receptacle wherein the Divine spirit can reside. Is this not good reason for joy?"

The Baal Shem Tov was elated with the *chazzan's* perspective on *teshuvah,* which is that rather than resulting in dejection, focusing on one's sins in order to eliminate them and beautify oneself to receive G-d's presence is uplifting.

When the Gaon of Vilna was in his last moments, he wept saying, "I know I am going to the bliss of *Gan Eden* (Paradise) but it is so painful to leave the world where for a few cents one can perform a mitzvah, something which is impossible to do in the Eternal World." If we truly appreciated the unparalleled value of mitzvos and realize that every day we have the opportunity to do many mitzvos, how great would be our joy!

None of us can approach the sublime spirituality of the Gaon or other great *tzaddikim,* whose grasp of Torah and mitzvos was so great that it obscured everything else and rendered all earthly concerns trivia. Yet, we should not resign ourselves to be helpless pawns, moved about by circumstances over which we have no control. A true trust in Hashem can help us overcome the impact of adversities on our mood.

There is a well-known story about a person who asked the Maggid of Mezeritch how the Talmud could demand of a person to be thankful to Hashem for the bad things that happened to him (Berachos 54a). The Maggid referred him to Rabbi Zusia for an answer.

Rabbi Zusia was a Talmudic scholar who concealed his knowledge of Torah, and gave the impression of being unlearned. Hence, when the man posed this question to him, he responded, "Why do you ask me? I am not well versed in Torah." When the man stated that the Maggid had referred him to the latter, Rabbi Zusia, shrugged his shoulders and said, "How can I answer that question? I have never experienced anything bad happening to me."

The man looked at Rabbi Zusia, whose tattered clothes tes-tified to his poverty, and who was stricken with a painful disease, and realized that his question had been answered.

On another occasion someone asked Rabbi Zusia, "How can you say the berachah, thanking G-d for providing for all your needs, when you are so impoverished that many of your needs are unmet? Don't you think you are dissim-ulating when you say this berachah?" Rabbi Zusia responded, "Not at all. G-d has a much better understand-ing of my needs than I do, and He understands that poverty is one of my needs."

Even if we cannot achieve the profound *emunah* of Rabbi Zusia, we should try to strengthen our *emunah* through study of Torah and learning from the lives of our great *tzaddikim*. The stronger our *emunah*, the less we will be upset when things do not go our way, and the more we will be able to generate *simchah*. But working toward greater *emunah* requires a dedication of *mesiras nefesh*.

We have noted that *living mesiras nefesh* is inavariably ben-eficial, and achieving *simchah* is certainly no exception. Many reliable medical studies stress the importance of attitude and mood for health and their impact on recovery from disease. There is valid evidence of cases where people have essentially laughed their way out of diseases for which there was no effec-tive treatment. The *mesiras nefesh* to attain a quality of *emunah* that will allow us to have an upbeat attitude of *simchah* will re-ward us handsomely with good health and success in our endeavors.

All for One
and One for All

One of the last acts of Moses was to assemble all of the Israelites to enter into a covenant of *areivus,* mutual responsibility. Although each person has an individual interest in life, the interest of *klal Yisrael,* the entire House of Israel, should override our individual interests. *Ahavas Yisrael,* love of a fellow Jew, is a mitzvah of the highest order, but does not yet confer any responsibility for the actions of another person. *Areivus* means that one cannot stand aside and assume that one does not affect others or is unaffected by them. The House of Israel is like one body, if something affects one part of the body, it affects the entire body.

I have learned a great deal from my work with recovering alcoholics. In our rehabilitation center, we would have weekly community meetings with everyone in the building in attendance: the clients, the therapists, the clerical staff, and the housekeeping personnel. The purpose of the meeting was to discuss whatever was occurring within the facility that might have an effect on anyone. This meeting was known as "bus stop," with the derivation of the name coming from the bus station, where many people may congregate in the same building, each one concerned only with getting to his own particular destination, and not concerned in the least where anyone else was going. The theme of the meeting was: Are we indeed a bus station, with everyone here seeking only to better himself/herself, or are we interdependent, with everyone's progress in recovery impacting in one way or another on everyone else?

The assumption was that these community meetings would foster a sense of interdependence, so that no one would isolate himself and consider himself separate from the group as a whole.

I was privileged to observe the development of a sense of mutual responsibility. Clients became interested in each other and were willing to help one another in whatever way possible. The attitude that prevailed was that "My recovery is incomplete if I stand apart from others." If a client wished to leave treatment prematurely, others would gather to discourage him from doing so. They frankly stated that their motivation was not purely altruistic, and that they felt that any person's failure to recover would have a negative effect on their personal recovery. There was a feeling in the group that they would either rise together or fall together.

There is a fable about a lion who caught a mouse. The mouse pleaded for its life, saying "If you release me, I will one day help you." The lion roared with laughter. "You are going to help me? I am the king of all animals. I am the mightiest of all in the jungle, and I certainly do not need the help of a lowly mouse." Nevertheless, the lion let him go. Some time later, the lion found himself trapped in a hunter's net and was unable to break loose. The mouse appeared, and said, "I will gnaw through the ropes and set you free." The mighty lion then realized that even he could not be totally self-sufficient, and needed to be rescued by the humble mouse.

This is what Moses intended with the covenant of *areivus*. Israel was not to be fragmented. One cannot drill a hole under one's own seat in a boat and claim that it is no one else's business.

There is a *Midrash* that is subject to misinterpretation. The *Midrash* states, "You, Israel, are referred to as *adam* (a person), and there are no other peoples in the world who can be referred to as *adam*." Some have sought to interpret this *Midrash* as being discriminating against non-Jews. During the Beiliss trial, when Jews all over the world were alarmed by the anti-Semitic blood libel against Mendel Beiliss, Rabbi Meir Shapiro of Lublin explained the *Midrash*. Jews the world over are as one person. Just as if a person hurts his toe, the entire body feels the pain, so if one Jew anywhere in the world is harmed, the pain is felt by Jews everywhere, even thousands of miles away. No other people has this sensitivity for one another.

Regardless to what degree a person manifests his Jewishness, there is a core of Jewishness in everyone, a spark which bursts into flame when Jews anywhere are threatened.

It is important that this sense of mutual responsibility be cultivated. The Talmud states that when Ahasuerus gave Haman his signet ring and authorized him to issue decrees at his whim, this threat was more effective in bringing Jews to *teshuvah* than the admonitions of 48 prophets. We find this very much true today in Israel. When anyone in Israel is threatened by its enemies, all divisiveness evaporates, and the entire population coalesces into one body.

Let us not wait for threats to bring us to our senses. Let us recognize that we are not only one nation but essentially one body.

It is of course much easier to insulate oneself, being responsible only for one's own actions and looking out only for one's own needs. To accept responsibility for others is indeed stressful, and requires a *living mesiras nefesh*. However, failure to do so results in fragmentation, which undermines the mission of Israel as expressed by the prophet, "For who is like Your people, Israel, one nation in the land" (*I Chronicles* 17:21).

On the Alert

Y ou will recall our discussion concerning operating on "manual" rather than on "automatic." Manual operation allows and requires a person to be ever on the alert.

People who are committed to Torah observance consider themselves to be *shomrei Torah*, or guardians of Torah. One of our great *tzaddikim* used to stay awake throughout the entire Shabbos, stating that he wished to be a true *shomer Shabbos*, and in view of the fact that a *shomer* or guard must not fall asleep while on sentry duty, neither can he, as a *shomer Shabbos,* be derelict in his obligations, which would happen if he were to sleep. If so, then as *shomrei Torah* we must be constantly on the alert.

We are not of the stature of the great *tzaddik*, and we cannot deny ourselves the sleep necessary for good health and optimal function. However, during our waking hours, we should be on the alert.

The *Shulchan Aruch* (Code of Jewish Law) begins with the verse "G-d is always before my eyes" (*Psalms* 16:8), and explains that a person behaves differently when in the presence of a king than he would in his own private chambers. We are to remember at all times that we are in the presence of G-d and act accordingly.

In the Torah we read about the temptation of Joseph, and how he resisted seduction (*Genesis* 39:7-13). The *Midrash* states that one of the factors that enabled Joseph to resist temptation was the thought that at any moment he might be visited by the Divine spirit, and how could he possibly permit himself to be in a state of defilement, which would render him unable to receive the presence of G-d?

We can find G-d not only in prayer and in Torah study, but everywhere in nature. Indeed, the section of the morning service preceding the *Shema* is devoted to recognizing G-d in the magnificent works of nature.

Being on the alert also enables us to constantly improve ourselves as we observe the world about us. The Talmud states that if the Torah had not been given, we would have been obligated to learn proper behavior by observing other creatures. Thus, we were to have learned respect for private property by observing that ants will not touch a morsel of food that was in the possession of another ant. We were to have learned marital fidelity by observing doves, who are monogamous. We were to have learned modesty from cats, who are discreet. Thus, even without Torah we are held to a standard of awareness so that we can learn proper behavior (*Eruvin* 100b). How much more so now that we have the charge of Torah to be a "kingdom of priests and a sacred nation" (*Exodus* 19:6)!

The Talmud states that if a person is engrossed in Torah study while he is walking, and interrupts his study to marvel at the beauty of a tree, it is as though he committed a sin which is deserving of the death punishment (*Ethics of the Fathers* 3:9). Why does the Talmud deal so harshly with this person? The answer is that marveling at a work of nature should not constitute an interruption of Torah study. To the contrary, someone who perceives the beauty of a tree, and understands that this magnificent tree grew out of a single seed which disintegrated in the soil and gave rise to a sapling, which then grew to its present stature, and particularly if one understands the highly complex structure of a single leaf, with the myriad channels whereby the nutrients are distributed, and how photosynthesis operates to convert simple minerals into complex organic structures which result in beautiful foliage and/or tasty fruit, this perception and contemplation should give rise to an awareness of the grandiosity of the Creator Who brought about this miracle. In other words, perceiving a beautiful tree should enhance one's Torah study rather than constitute an interruption. If a person fails to see the greatness of G-d in nature, and restricts G-dliness to religious ritual rather than to everything in the universe, he is indeed guilty of a grave sin. Everything we perceive in the world should be a testimony to the glory of G-d.

*A*n example of alertness is the anecdote of Rabbi *Yisrael of Salant, who, while walking with several students, noted a procession of three horses drawing wagons laden with hay. Rabbi Yisrael pointed out that the lead horse has the benefit that his load is constantly becoming lighter as the middle horse eats from it, but he does not have any hay before him to eat. The last horse, on the other hand, can eat from the wagon before him, but his load never gets any lighter. The middle horse has the best of all possible worlds, in that he can eat and also has his load lessened.*

"This proves to you the validity of the Rambam's teaching," Rabbi Yisrael said, "that one should always follow the middle path and avoid either extreme. The

middle horse has the maximum advantage, while those at either extreme are at some disadvantage."

There are people who can sit through a lecture on *mussar* and fail to be impressed, whereas Rabbi Yisrael can see a procession of horses and derive a valuable lesson in behavior.

Another aspect of being on the alert is to always be aware of the need to improve oneself, and be willing to learn from everyone, as the psalmist says, "I learned from all my teachers" (*Psalms* 119:99), and the Talmud points out that one can learn more from one's students than from peers and even teachers.

A woman once came to Rabbi Aryeh Levin, complaining that her husband was not treating her respectfully, and she asked the rabbi to reprimand him. Rabbi Levin felt that to do so would only put him on the defensive and that he might act out against his wife for having maligned him before the rabbi. He therefore decided to wait until the husband was in attendance at one of his Torah study classes, at which time he would elaborate on the importance of proper domestic conduct.

Before long this opportunity arose, and Rabbi Aryeh used the portion of the Torah being studied as a springboard from which he was able to expand on the teachings of the Talmud, that a husband must accord his wife even greater respect than he would demand for himself, and that it is a grave sin to act towards one's wife in a manner that offends her dignity. He went into great detail, citing numerous authorities on the subject, and giving examples of how our great Torah personalities exercised the utmost caution in being sensitive to their wives' emotional needs.

After the session was over, Rabbi Isser Zalman Meltzer, who was Rabbi Levin's teacher and mentor, and who was in shul and overheard the discussion, approached Rabbi Levin and thanked him. "I am so grateful that you brought this to my attention," he said. "Perhaps I have not been as sensitive to my wife's needs as I should have been."

Whether the husband of the woman who complained to Rabbi Levin got the message is questionable. He might not even have appreciated that it was directed to him. On the other hand, the great *tzaddik*, whose behavior towards his wife was undoubtedly exemplary, was the one who took the message to heart. We would do well to emulate the *tzaddik* and always be on the alert for ways in which we might improve ourselves.

How much of a state of readiness we maintain may serve as an indication of the degree of our commitment to the Divine service. A businessman who is interested in increasing the profitability of his concern is constantly on the lookout for ways in which he can make more money. He is ever on the alert for ways in which to attract new customers, better market his product, or improve his product to be more salable. He is likely to be quite distressed if he were to let an opportunity slip by him. It is not unusual for him to take his business concerns with him up to the very moment he falls asleep, and his dreams may even be about his business. He hardly considers this attitude to be a sacrifice, because the success of his business is of overriding importance to him. The improvement of one's character and a more perfect performance of mitzvos should be no less important than the success of one's business.

Is it comfortable to be on constant alert? Of course not. It is far more comfortable to operate on "automatic." However, if one aspires to become everything that a person can become, one will have the requisite *mesiras nefesh* to forgo the comfort and strive for greater spiritual achievement.

Maintaining Sensitivity

We relate to the world about us through our senses, receiving information primarily via our eyes and ears. This information is then processed by our intellect, but our cognition, or knowledge of things, is profoundly affected by our emotions. It is generally accepted that emotions influence our judgment, and this is why a judge is forbidden to take a bribe. It is not as readily appreciated that emotions may also affect our perception of things. In the prohibition against taking a bribe, the Torah states, "because a bribe can *blind* the eyes of the wise and distort the words of the just" (*Deuteronomy* 16:19); i.e., a bribe not only distorts the thought processes but can also render the judge oblivious to the facts presented to him.

We must exert utmost caution when we try to analyze the behavior of the personalities of the Scriptures. Although they were human beings, they were so far advanced spiritually that they differ from us quantitatively rather than just qualitatively. We can look at them only through the eyes of our Torah authorities, whose grasp of what these great people were like is more valid than ours.

The Torah tells us that when there was a hunger in Canaan, Abraham went to Egypt, and because he feared that the Egyptians might kill him in order to take Sarah, he said that she was his sister rather than his wife. Ramban states that the Patriarch inadvertently committed a great wrong by going to Egypt and by jeopardizing the safety of his wife, and that he should have trusted in G–d and remained where he was (*Genesis* 12:10).

Rabbi Yehudah Leib Chasman states that Ramban must have received this interpretation as a Divine inspiration, because on his own he would never had made a critical comment about the Patriarch. What the Torah is teaching us with this episode, however, is that even someone as spiritually advanced as the Patriarch Abraham is vulnerable to making a mistake in judgment when a personal interest is involved (*Ohr Yahel* Volume 3, page 30-32).

Rabbi Chasman points out that this teaching is nothing less than awesome. The Patriarch Abraham — who accepted martyrdom and was thrown into a fiery furnace by Nimrod for his refusal to acknowledge paganism, and who withstood ten trials, including the willingness to bring his beloved son Isaac as an offering — erred, on his level, which Ramban says, was one of the reasons his descendants were sentenced to enslavement in Egypt.

What we must learn from this is that no one is immune, and regardless of how objective we may think ourselves to be, we are all vulnerable to misjudgments. The latter may come about when we have a personal interest in what the outcome of the decision will be, and even the saintly Patriarch was unable to judge correctly because of personal interest.

If it were not that Ramban made this statement, and the great ethicist elaborated on it, we would not be in a position to analyze the judgment of the Patriarch. But since these Torah authorities have given us this interpretation, we must use it as a guide for ourselves, and always be alert to the susceptibility to err in judgment, regardless of how certain we may be about the correctness of our decision.

Many times during each day we make decisions, and each time we make a decision we are acting as a judge weighing the pros and cons of each situation. Should I, or should I not? Will this be to my advantage or a detriment? We may even be on our guard, realizing that we are tempted to decide in favor of whatever would be most pleasing or least distressing for us. We may not, however, consider the possibility that we are not in possession of all the facts involved, because our perceptions as well as our judgment has been affected by our desires. While it is an overgeneralization to say that we see what we wish to see and hear what we wish to hear, an honest self-examination will reveal that this does indeed occur.

We are warned about this by the prophet, who says, "The heart of this nation has become fattened, their ears heavy, and their eyes sealed, lest they see with their eyes, hear with their ears, and understand with their hearts so that they will repent and be healed" (Isaiah 6:10). It could not be stated more clearly: If seeing and hearing may result in the need to change, we may become selectively blind and deaf.

Clinically, I have repeatedly encountered incidents of absolute *denial*, wherein a person who is confronted with incontrovertible facts simply does not see them This is classic in the case of the alcoholic, whose job, family, and health may be disintegrating right before his eyes, and although this is repeatedly pointed out to him, he simply fails to see it.

Inasmuch as we are all subject to the influences of various emotions, we should be aware that we are subject to this psychological phenomenon, whereby we may be rendered insensitive to things, the awareness of which might cause us some discomfort.

Rabbi Chaim Shmulevitz provides us with some striking examples of these phenomena. He cites the Scriptural account of Chiel, who defied Joshua's curse that whoever rebuilt Jericho would suffer the loss of his children. Chiel's eldest son died when Chiel laid the foundation of Jericho, and one by one, his children continued dying until his youngest child died when the gates of the city were erected. Rabbi Shmulevitz points out that there was no way he could avoid seeing what was happening, unless he was blinded by his drive to rebuild the city, so blinded that he did not perceive what should have been blatantly evident to him (*Sichos Mussar* 7, 5732).

There is another type of insensitivity that may distort our perception and judgment, and that is our becoming accustomed to something. Indeed, the Talmud states that when a person repeats a misdeed, he soon fails to see that it is wrong, even if he initially had recognized this (*Moed Kattan* 27a). This is true not only of something that we may do, but also of things that we may see or hear, which may be shocking or revolting to us upon our first encounter, but may lose their opprobrium with repeated exposure. We have witnessed this phenomenon in a rather recent event, wherein the participation of a physician in helping a person take his own life was greeted with an expression of outrage, only to fade into virtual acceptance as the incidents were repeated, to the point where courts and legislatures have begun to deliberate the legitimacy of physician-assisted suicide.

Rabbi Shmulevitz cites the *Midrash* which relates that when the Patriarch Jacob's children brought him to burial in the cave of Machpelah, Esau protested, claiming that Jacob had no rights to this site. The sons disputed the issue with Esau, who demanded to see Jacob's deed to the property, which had remained in Egypt. Naftali, who was a swift runner, was dispatched to bring the document. Hushim, the son of Dan, who was deaf and was not privy to the negotiations, asked why Jacob's burial was being delayed, and when told that they were awaiting Naftali's return in order to refute Esau, Hushim remarked, "What! And until then our grandfather shall suffer the disgrace of not being buried?" whereupon he killed Esau.

"Why did the others in attendance not kill Esau?" Rabbi Shmulevitz asks. "Were they not as concerned about Jacob's honor as Hushim?" And he answers, "Indeed they were, but because they had entered into a dispute with Esau and had been involved in the arguments, the initial shock wore off, and they no longer felt the dishonor as keenly as did Hushim, whose inability to hear prevented him from participating in the proceedings. Hushim never lost his sensitivity, and reacted with horror when he discovered what was happening" (*ibid.* 32, 5731).

We are exposed, as never before in history, to accounts of immorality, indecency, violence, and atrocities. These are brought into the living room or to the dinner table by television newscasts, and even homes that are free of television cannot escape the impact of the mass media. Nothing is shocking any more. Repeated exposure has rendered us relatively indifferent to many evils, if not frankly calloused.

I have often encountered this apparent contradiction clinically in my treatment of drug users. Young people who have witnessed friends die of heroin or cocaine have a delusion of immunity. They may actually rationalize their further use by explaining that their friends died because of reckless use, whereas they will be more careful and will avoid the disastrous effects of the drug. They may give themselves a false sense of security, and rather than concluding from their friends' death that the drugs are lethal, instead conclude that they themselves have learned how to use drugs safely.

This warped thinking was described by the Talmud. Following the humiliating ritual of the adulterous woman, the Torah gives the rules for a nazirite, who takes upon himself a period of mandatory abstention from wine. The Talmud states that these verses are juxtaposed, so that "one who has witnessed the humiliation of the adulterous woman will beware of the intoxicating effects of wine" (*Sotah* 2a), because it is the latter that leads to indecent behavior. This extra warning is necessary for someone who has witnessed the humiliation because he is likely to have a false sense of security, and like the drug addict, may think that his exposure to the harmful consequences of intoxication have given him stronger defenses against them.

Sensitivity has its price. When I acquired my first stereo (then it was known as a hi-fi phonograph), I was delighted with the quality of the sound, but I found that when I walked into the room, the vibrations of my steps caused the needle to jump the groove on the record. Because of the exquisite sensitivity of the instrument, it was much more delicate, and I had to tread softly to avoid upsetting it. The old phonograph never demanded such delicate handling, but its sound reproduction was vastly inferior. Thus it was a tossup between better sound or lesser painstaking walking.

We often find ourselves in situations where heightened sensitivity causes us discomfort, and it requires a degree of *mesiras nefesh* to maintain this sensitivity. However, if we are to be the spiritual people we were meant to be, we dare not allow ourselves to become indifferent.

We can bring comfort to others by sharing in their distress, not only because "a sorrow shared is halved," but also because it may result in an actual alleviation of the other person's burden. The chassidic master, Rabbi Elimelech of Lizensk, explained it this way. The Divine wisdom may have decreed, for reasons known only to G–d, that Reuvain must experience suffering. Reuvain shares his plight with Shimon, and Shimon so empathizes and identifies with Reuvain that he, too, feels the distress and suffers along with him. However, since the Divine decree was not that Shimon should suffer, G–d must relieve Reuvain's distress in order to spare Shimon unjust suffering. Therefore, said Rabbi Elimelech, when you truly feel for someone who is suffering, you may be the catalyst for his being relieved. Granted that it is uncomfortable to so identify with someone that you feel his pain, but how wonderful and uplifting a feeling it is to know that you may be mitigating his distress.

The *Midrash* states that when Moses went out among his enslaved brethren in Egypt, he placed his shoulder under their heavy loads. How much actual help could he be to the tens of thousands of slaves? The point was that he did not stand aside, but did something that would enable him to actually feel their pain, and this is why he was chosen to be the Deliverer. The Mishnah says that one of the prerequisites for acquisition of Torah is "to share in the burdens of others" (*Ethics of the Fathers* 6:6), and it was Moses' exquisite sensitivity in trying to actually feel the suffering of others that merited his becoming the receiver of Torah par excellence.

This sensitivity must also characterize any actions one takes to correct or reprimand others. Although we may wish to help people adopt a life-style which we consider to be the appropriate one for a Jew, we must never lose sight of the fact that any kind of admonishment, even when well intended, can be distressful. We have already pointed out that we must never say or do anything that will humiliate someone publicly. But even when done in private, we must be cautious to relate to others in such a manner that they do not feel hurt, and we can do this only if we are sensitive to others' feelings.

We know that giving *tzedakah* is one of the greatest mitzvos in the Torah. Yet there is something that surpasses even *tzedakah*, and that is *gemillas chessed*, doing personal acts of kindness. It is indeed very meritorious to write out a check to a charitable organization, but doing personal acts of kindness allows us to become involved with those who need help, to feel for them and with them, which helps us avoid the numbing effects of modern living and maintain our sensitivity.

Concern for G–d

t is difficult to look away from one's own needs. When we pray, we ask G–d to give us good health, an adequate livelihood, and *nachas* from our loved ones. As virtuous as this prayer may be, because it testifies to our awareness that all our blessings flow from G–d and that we are dependent upon Him, the works of *chassidus* and *mussar* tell us that it is not yet the finest of prayers. We achieve the latter when we pray not for ourselves, but for G–d.

Pray for G–d? That seems absurd! G–d lacks for nothing. But the psalmist has set the tone for the ideal prayer. "Not for our sake, Hashem, not for our sake, but for Your Name's sake give glory . . . Why should the nations of the world say, 'Where now is their G–d'?" (*Psalms* 115:1). When Jews suffer persecution, other nations may say that G–d cannot protect them, and this is insulting to G–d. It was this argument that won forgiveness for the Israelites when they committed the sin of worshipping the golden calf (*Exodus* 32:12), and again when they refused to enter the Promised Land (*Numbers* 14:16). In both instances Moses pleaded that there would be a *chilul Hashem*, a dishonor of the Divine Name, if G–d were to inflict His wrath upon the Israelites.

In treating young addicts, I often advise parents that in order to arrest the progression of drug addiction in their adolescent children, they must adopt an attitude of "tough love," which means that they must take harsh measures so that the youngster will come to his senses and not destroy himself with drugs. This may require establishing the rule that "our home is drug free," and that while they cannot stop the youngster from using drugs, he must understand that he cannot live at home if he persists in doing so. This may require expelling him from the house, changing the locks on the doors, and making it clear to him that he will be arrested if he tries to enter the house by force. Parents are understandably loathe to take so radical a step, but when they realize that this is what it may take to stop the youngster's self-destruction, they do what they must. I can assure you that the pain experienced by parents who lock their child out of their home is far greater than that of the youngster who finds himself on the street. The child invariably finds drug-using friends with whom he can stay, and it is the parents who have sleepless nights and suffer the torment of their child having been expelled.

It is at times like these that I feel that perhaps I can begin to understand the agony of G–d, Who expelled us from our homeland because of our dereliction in observing the Torah. Deviation from the Torah is self-destructive, and G–d made it clear in the Torah that if we engaged in self-destructive behavior, we would be expelled. For all the persecutions we have suffered, we have nevertheless adjusted to exile, often living quite comfortably away from our home, and we may not feel the pain of exile. It is G–d, our Father, Who is unconsolable, and Who suffers the agony of having expelled us from our home.

Why does G–d not simply relieve His agony by bringing us back? For the same reason that parents cannot take back a wayward child until he has abandoned his self-destructive behavior. Although G–d controls everything, He has divested Himself of controlling our moral and ethical behavior. This is something which man himself must do , and we are totally free to choose between good and evil. If we do choose to do wrong, G–d will not intervene to stop us, but will exert appropriate disciplinary action which, even far more than human parents, causes Him much agony.

Rabbi Yehoshua Leib Diskin was the chief rabbi of Jerusalem, and his residence was extremely tiny and very sparsely furnished, hardly what one would expect for a person who occupied so prominent and distinguished a position. One time a visitor remarked to him that it was really not proper for so important a personage to be living in such meager surroundings. Rabbi Yehoshua Leib opened the window which faced the mountain site where the Temple had once stood. Tearfully he remarked, "G–d's Home is in ruin. Do I have the right to live in more lavish surroundings?"

In an earlier discussion of prayer, we noted that we must pray for others as well as for ourselves. The finest of all prayers is when we sincerely pray for Divine help so that G–d will be spared the distress when He commiserates with us, as the psalmist says, "I am with him in ther anguish" (*Psalms* 91:15).

A chassid who dealt in lumber complained to his Rebbe that he had bought a forest, but that the price of lumber declined, and he sustained a severe financial loss. The Rebbe replied, "When you are in anguish, G–d suffers along with you. Now tell me, is it worthwhile to inflict suffering upon G–d because of a few pieces of wood? If you can accept this reversal with serenity, you will be sparing G–d from agonizing along with you."

Incidentally, when we pray for G–d rather than for ourselves, our prayers are especially effective. When we ask for personal needs, our records are likely to be reviewed to determine whether we are deserving of special favors. When we pray for G–d, no such scrutiny occurs.

Mesiras nefesh is usually associated with *kiddush Hashem,* sanctifying the Divine Name. While this often refers to martyrdom, we have emphasized the application of the term to living rather than to dying. Setting one's own needs and wishes aside in order to pray for G–d is indeed an act of *mesiras nefesh,* and because these prayers are so effective, they will result in bringing honor to G–d, which is the goal of *kiddush Hashem.*

The Torah as a Blueprint

O n several occasions we have referred to *living mesiras nefesh* as actually being in one's self-interest rather than being a sacrifice. We can have a more comprehensive grasp of this if we have a better understanding of the nature of Torah.

It is possible to be fully observant of Torah and mitzvos, and even have a deep *yiras shamayim*, reverence for G–d, and yet fail to understand what commitment to Torah really means. We may be loyal to G–d and obey His commandments like a soldier who obeys his commanding officer, whether out of respect for him or fear of repercussions if he violates a command. While this is certainly commendable, it is not yet ideal.

The *Zohar* states that G–d "gazed at the Torah and created the world." In other words, the Torah is not something that was superimposed upon the world when it was given at Sinai. Rather, the world was created on the basis of Torah and operates according to Torah principles. The "laws" of Torah are not laws in the sense of legislation, but rather in the sense of laws of nature. It is related that at one meeting of a congressional finance committee someone objected to a particular proposal, citing Gresham's law that "bad money pushes good money out of circulation," whereupon a rather uneducated member said, "That should not stand in our way. We are Congress. Let's just repeal Gresham's law." He was unaware that Gresham's law is no more subject to repeal than is the law of gravity. Torah laws must be understood as being laws of nature and, much like the law of gravity, cannot be repealed nor modified.

Conceptualized in this way, we can appreciate that Torah is reality and that Torah cannot be defied any more than one can defy reality. People who defy reality invariably suffer the consequences, and this is equally true of those who defy Torah.

This principle is explained by Rabbi Chaim Shmulevitz, who cites the Talmudic statement that Moses was angry on three occasions, and each time erred in judgment, as the Talmud states, "If one is enraged, he loses his prophecy if he is a prophet, or loses his wisdom if he is wise." Rabbi Shmulevitz points out that Moses was perfectly justified in his anger, but that the consequences of rage are not different whether or not the anger is justified. A person may be perfectly justified in putting his hand in a flame to save something valuable, but the fire will burn his hand nevertheless. The impairment of judgment which Moses experienced was not a Divine punishment for his being angry, since he had every reason to be angry. Rather, the momentary loss of wisdom was a natural consequence of the law of nature, according to which anger has deleterious consequences.

We perceive reality via our senses, but that Torah is reality is not a sense experience. Rather it is a matter of *emunah*, a conviction of faith. To the degree that we have this conviction, to that degree we can orient our lives. It is then as patently absurd to try to modify Torah laws or to try to circumvent them in any way as it is to jump out the window and hope to circumvent the law of gravity because one thinks one has found a loophole therein.

The Talmud relates that King Solomon tried to circumvent Torah and failed. The Torah states that a king should not have too many wives, lest they deter him from full adherence to Torah. Solomon was so certain of the strength of his faith and dedication to Torah that he felt he was not subject to this risk, and took more wives than the Torah prescribed. G–d said, "Not a single letter of the Torah will ever be futile," and the great Solomon did indeed experience detrimental consequences (*Sanhedrin* 21b). No one, not even the wisest of men, can alter the reality of Torah.

The Maggid of Koznitz once arose from the Shabbos table and inadvertently jarred the table slightly, causing a candle to fall from its holder and extinguish, whereupon he began crying bitterly. When it was pointed out to him that this was completely unintentional and that there was no reason for him to feel guilty about so accidental a happening, the Maggid remarked, "I am not concerned about this act. However, the Talmud states that 'a sin begets a sin,' and even though this sin was innocent and I may not be culpable for it, I am afraid of what it might bring in its wake."

The *Maggid* understood the Talmudic statement to be a law of nature, and even an "innocent" sin for which one may not be culpable can give rise to a more serious transgression.

I have learned some valuable lessons from working with alcoholics. I instruct people in recovery to avoid even the slightest amount of alcohol, since it has been conclusively established that even one drink can set into motion a destructive cycle. One time I received a panicky call from a man who was in the early stages of recovery, and who had been threatened with the loss of his job if he relapsed. He had been invited to a friend's celebration, and refused the offer of a drink, but did take some punch. The first taste of the punch revealed that it had been spiked with alcohol, whereupon he promptly put it down and called me to find out what he must do to prevent this accidental consumption of a few drops of alcohol from escalating into a full-scale relapse. He had come to realize from his previous efforts at trying to control his drinking that "alcohol begets alcohol" is a fact of nature. We must also understand that "sin begets sin" is not an abstract concept or merely an admonition, but is an incontrovertible law of nature.

We are immediately aware of the body, and that exposing the body to noxious substances causes harm. Taking into account that the *neshamah* is intangible and not immediately evident to us, we are not as likely to be aware of things that damage it. It is, however, a fact of nature that transgression of Torah damages the *neshamah*. If we truly value the *neshamah*, we would be as cautious in protecting it from harm as we are of protecting the body from injury.

We can now see why *mesiras nefesh* is really not a sacrifice. A person who is diabetic and who is tempted by a rich dessert will exercise restraint because he wishes to preserve his health, and one would hardly consider this restraint to be a sacrifice. To the contrary, we would consider his yielding to temptation to be foolish and reckless. Similarly, a firm conviction of the reality of the *neshamah* and of Torah should make us realize that depriving ourselves of some things we may desire or exerting ourselves in the way Torah requires is hardly a sacrifice. We are simply protecting ourselves from harm.

Preserving
the Awakening

here is yet another similarity between a *living mesiras nefesh* and that of martyrdom. We are familiar with incidents of people who led lives of sin, but died with an attitude of sincere repentance. One such case related in the Talmud is that of Elazar ben Doradia, a reprobate of unspeakable immorality, who abruptly repented his past and wept so bitterly over his past that he died while crying. A voice from heaven proclaimed that Elazar ben Doradia merited Paradise, which caused Rabbi Yehudah HaNasi to weep, saying, "One can acquire the Eternal World in a brief period of time" (*Avodah Zarah* 17a) True, Elazar had redeemed himself, but moments of spiritual awakening need not come so late in life and after so much improper behavior that one cannot live with the redemption.

We all have moments of spiritual arousal. The Baal ShemTov stated that there is a heavenly voice that calls people to do *teshuvah*, and that although it is not audible to our ears, the *neshamah* does hear it, and when we have moments of spiritual arousal, it is because the *neshamah* has heard this Divine call. The problem is that we may overlook this opportunity to respond to the heavenly call.

It is not uncommon to set the alarm clock to wake up at a certain time, but when the alarm sounds, one may turn it off for "just a few more moments of sleep," only to discover much later that one had overslept. If one must make an early morning flight which one cannot afford to miss, one may take the precaution of removing the alarm clock from the nightstand and placing it in a remote corner of the room so that one cannot turn it off while in bed. In this way, one makes sure that the arousal achieves its purpose.

We would be wise to do something similar to preserve these precious moments of spiritual awakening rather than allowing them to fade as we resume our regular routine. One might capture the arousal by doing a mitzvah, such as giving *tzedakah*, or reciting a few chapters of *Tehillim*, or learning a *mishnah*. Any mitzvah can preserve the moment of arousal, so that we can engage it to enhance the spiritual quality of our lives. In this way, Rabbi Yehudah HaNasi's statement that "one can acquire the Eternal World in a brief period of time" can be said with joy instead of with tears. To seize and preserve these precious moments of arousal, which are Divine gifts, requires that we be in a state of alertness, operating on "manual," because otherwise we are likely to turn off the spiritual "alarm clock" and go back to the slumber of habit and routine. Giving up the comfort of the latter requires a living *mesiras nefesh*.

There is a common trait which militates against our seizing the moment of spiritual arousal, and that is *procrastination*. RaMCHaL in *The Path of The Just* devotes an entire section to the trait of *zerizus* (diligence or zeal). *Zerizus* is an essential step in ascending the ladder of spirituality, and it is the antithesis of procrastination. The Talmud states, "when the opportunity presents itself to do a mitzvah, do not postpone it" (*Rashi, Exodus* 12:17), and "If you find a reason to be idle of Torah once, you will find many reasons to extend the idleness" (*Ethics of the Fathers* 4:10). Experience has more than proven the truth of this statement: Once we begin postponing something, we are likely to continue postponing it.

A tzaddik was invited to an early-morning bris (circumcision), but came quite late and apologized for his tardiness, stating that he was learning Torah through the night and fell asleep just before dawn. Someone remarked, "Why didn't you go to sleep earlier, and get up early in the morning to learn?" The tzaddik responded, "What assurance did I have that I would even wake up in the morning?" The present moment is the only one we know we can use. No one can know what lies ahead in the future.

In my treatment of alcoholics I have seen people who have made a radical change in their lives, but too often this occurs only after decades of devastation, leaving behind shattered lives. When these people see a young person enter treatment, they invariably say, "I wish I could have come to my senses when I was young. I could have spared myself and others all the misery I wrought with my drinking." While I am pleased to witness recovery at any age, I can identify with Rabbi Yehudah HaNasi who wept upon hearing of Elazar ben Doradia's repentance. How much harm would have been avoided had he come to this realization earlier!

All That
One Can Be

Perhaps the greatest challenge that confronts a person, and which requires *mesiras nefesh*, is to become all that one can become, to fulfill one's potential. Our great Torah personalities, who were well aware of their erudition in Torah, were nevertheless humbled by their awareness that their great achievements notwithstanding, they had not fulfilled their potential.

There is the well-known anecdote of the chassidic master, Rabbi Zusia, who said, "I am not afraid of being asked on Judgment Day why I was not as great as the Baal Shem Tov, because I will say, 'How could you even expect me to be as great as the Baal Shem Tov?' And for the same reason I will not be afraid if they ask me why I was not as great as the Maggid. But if they will say, 'Zusia! Why weren't you Zusia?' Then, woe is me! What justification can I give for my not having become all that I could have become if only I had tried harder?"

Without *mesiras nefesh* we are prone to accept our status quo as adequate. Many people can consider their life-style as being completely compatible with *halachah,* and may not realize that failure to grow spiritually is a dereliction in Torah observance.

It is related that the king of Prussia instructed the Crown Prince to wage war and annex a neighboring territory. When the Crown Prince asked why this was necessary, the king replied, "If you do not expand the nation's borders, they will recede." This may or may not be true in statesmanship, but it is certainly true in character development. We are not stagnant spiritually. If we do not advance, we regress.

There is an interesting *Midrash* which states that over each blade of grass there stands an angel who whips it and commands it to grow. Why is this necessary? Given that the seed lies in soil which has all the necessary nutrients, and there is sufficient water, growth is a natural and spontaneous phenomenon. The *Midrash* is telling us that this is not so. Even with all the ingredients being available, growth is *not* natural. To the contrary, the natural state of all matter is *inertia,* and there must be a force and drive to overcome the inertia. This is even more true of living things which, when satiated, assume a posture of rest and inaction. We would have to admit that we are often derelict in advancing ourselves. Can we truthfully say that our prayer today was with greater *kavannah* (concentration) than yesterday's prayer?

One might ask: Where in the Torah is there a requirement to advance oneself spiritually? In *Proverbs,* King Solomon repeatedly cites indolence as being one of the most destructive traits, and surrendering to inertia is nothing other than indolence. The *Midrash* states that Moses was referring to the need to overcome inertia when he said, "It (the Torah) is very near to you, in your mouth and in your heart to do it" (*Deuteronomy* 30:14). We thus have a Scriptural command to develop ourselves to our full potential.

How grave a transgression it is to fail to develop ourselves to our full potential can be seen from the Talmud, which relates that the disciples of Rabbi Eliezer came to visit him when he was sick, and the sage predicted that they would not die a natural death. (These disciples were the victims of Roman cruelty, and we lament their deaths in the liturgy of Tishah B'Av and Yom Kippur.) Rabbi Akiva asked the master, "What will my fate be?" and Rabbi Eliezer replied, "Your end will be more severe than the others, because your capacity for understanding Torah is very great, and had you remained closer to me you could have advanced much more in Torah" (*Sanhedrin* 68a). Rabbi Akiva's death was indeed most painful, as he was tortured to the very end.

The message of this episode is nothing less than startling. The great Rabbi Akiva, whose knowledge of and devotion to Torah surpassed anything that we can possibly imagine, was considered negligent because he could have become even greater!

We have noted earlier that *mesiras nefesh* is in fact not a sacrifice, because it is invariably to our own advantage. This is equally true of the extra effort one must make to break loose from the bonds of inertia. Let us compare the functioning of a four-cylinder automobile engine, which may generate 60 horsepower, to that of an eight-cylinder engine, which has two defective cylinders, so that it generates 180 horsepower instead of the 300 horsepower it could produce if all eight cylinders were operative. Although the larger engine generates three times as much power as the smaller one, the ride in the larger automobile will be quite uncomfortable, because the malfunction of the two cylinders will result in very annoying vibrations.

In the case of the automobile, it is the passenger who will feel the discomfort of the faulty engine. In the case of the human being, he is at once both the engine and the passenger. Failure to operate according to one's capacity will result in unpleasant sensations, which may manifest as emotional symptoms. While it is certainly true that some emotional feelings may be due to biochemical changes in the body which need to be corrected by treatment, it is also possible for a person to feel ill at ease because he is not living up to his full potential.

We noted earlier that if the Torah had not been given, we were expected to learn proper behavior from observation of nature. This principle still holds true, and we might gain much from studying the life cycle of lobsters.

Lobsters are creatures that live inside a rigid, unyielding shell, which does not grow much, if at all. As the lobster grows, it feels the discomfort of pressure within its confining shell. It then retreats into one of the underwater rock formations, sheds its shell, and produces a new one. This process is repeated several times until the lobster reaches its maximum size.

We should learn two things from this phenomenon. Firstly, that the discomfort the lobster feels is an indication that it is growing, and that it must rid itself of the restrictive shell in order to grow. If the lobster had the equivalent of valium, it might rid itself of the discomfort by taking a tranquilizer and remaining stunted rather than ridding itself of the restraining shell which restricts its growth. We should recognize that sometimes we may be ill at ease not because there is anything wrong with us, but that, like the eight cylinder engine that is lacking two functioning cylinders, we are not operating at our full potential, and that is causing us discomfort. Rather than numbing ourselves with tranquilizers, we ought to be stimulated to grow.

A second lesson we should derive from observing the lobster is that when it sheds its shell, it leaves itself vulnerable to predatory fish or to sudden surges of current which can crush it against a rock. In other words, a lobster must endure a life-threatening risk in order to grow. We are fortunate in that we do not have to risk our lives in order to grow, but we must be prepared to accept some stress in overcoming our natural inertia and elevating ourselves to a higher spiritual level.

To Thine Own Self Be True

The Torah states, "Do not deceive another person" (*Leviticus* 25:17), to which the Rabbi of Kotzk added, "And do not deceive yourself either." While deceiving another person is sinful, deceiving oneself is most foolish. What gain can there possibly be if a person is the victim of his own cunning?

Yet, self-deception is far from a rarity. We are quite prone to deceiving ourselves, primarily because we wish to interpret reality in such a way that it will provide us the utmost gratification.

Self-deception is particularly treacherous because we are virtually defenseless against it. If a person has succeeded in deceiving himself, he hardly knows that he is doing this. The only salvation would be for some outside observer to make him aware of this, but unfortunately, people often turn a deaf ear to those who wish to correct them.

How seriously the Torah considers self-deception is pointed out by Rabbi Chaim Shmulevitz in his discussion of the sin of usury. The Torah forbids taking interest for a personal loan, but whereas a person is granted the right on Judgment Day to present an argument in his defense for any other sins he committed, no arguments whatever may be offered in defense of someone who took interest. Think of it! This does not hold true for any other, even the most severe transgressions, where a plea for lenience may be entered. There is no lenience, however, for someone who took interest.

Rabbi Shmulevitz suggests that the reason the sin of usury is treated so harshly is because the lender is likely to be under the delusion that he has not sinned at all. To the contrary, he thinks he has done a mitzvah by lending the money. The borrower may have a poor credit rating and could not have obtained a loan elsewhere, and even if he did, the interest he would be charged would be exorbitant. Here he is lending his money at a lower interest rate than the borrower would pay elsewhere. Why, he is doing the person a great favor, and this should be considered a great mitzvah, shouldn't it?

No, says Rabbi Shmulevitz. The lender is profiting from the loan, and is taking the borrower's money unjustly, because he should be giving him an interest-free loan. Whereas a thief who takes someone else's money knows he is doing wrong, the lender deludes himself into thinking that he has actually done a mitzvah, and this is why no defense is permitted. The Torah wishes to alert a person to the evils of self-deception. A thief may suffer the pangs of a guilty conscience and do teshuvah, whereas one who lends on usury, who may have even received the gratitude of the borrower, is hardly likely to change his ways and do teshuvah for what he considers to have been a mitzvah.

Our tzaddikim were always on guard lest they delude themselves. They were supersensitive to the possibility that they might err in deciding what is a mitzvah and what is not.

The Maggid of Chernobel was approached by a man who asked for money for a dowry for his daughter, who would otherwise be unable to do a shidduch (matrimonial match). The man said that he needed 300 rubles. Later that day a wealthy chassid gave the Maggid a contribution of 300 rubles, and the Maggid was overjoyed that he would be able help this man marry off his daughter. A bit later the Maggid reflected whether it would not be more equitable if he gave this man 150 rubles, and distributed the remainder among other needy people, and this might be even a greater mitzvah. The Maggid was in a quandary because there were two possible things he could do, but only one was the appropriate one. He gave this much thought, and finally decided in favor of giving the entire sum to the man who needed the dowry. His reasoning was that this had been his first impulse, and it is characteristic for the first impulse to originate from the yetzer tov; the yetzer hara then tries to sabotage the yetzer tov's advice.

The point of this story for us is not which was actually the right decision, but rather that the tzaddik was on the alert that he not delude himself.

There is a greater risk of self-deception when one tries to be extra-pious, and this is why we must consult a Torah authority to make sure that what we are doing is indeed proper. We have already noted that self-imposed fasting is not recommended for everyone, and that mortification of the flesh may be counterproductive. The *Maggid* of Mezeritch cautioned that a small defect in the *guf* may result in a major defect in the *neshamah*. A person who thinks that fasting alone constitutes *teshuvah* is deluding himself, as the prophet says, "Do you call this a fast and a day of favor to G–d? The fast that G–d chooses is to release your bonds of wickedness" (*Isaiah* 58:5-6). Fasting is appropriate only as the icing on the cake, following sincere *teshuvah,* and when the latter is accomplished, fasting is often not necessary.

The psalmist says, "Guard my soul because I am pious" (*Psalms* 86:2). The question is obvious: Why does a pious person need special protection? *Bnei Yissaschor* explains that a person who is guided in his behavior by *halachah* is not likely to be confused and mistake an improper act for a mitzvah. All he needs to do is consult the *Shulchan Aruch,* which will tell him whether it is a mitzvah or not. The *chassid* or ultra-pious person wishes to do things that are not required by the *Shulchan Aruch* and hence do not appear there. He thus has no firm guidelines for his behavior, and it is possible that in his zeal he may do things which are improper, thinking them to be meritorious. This is why King David prayed, "Protect me from mistakes that I might make because I am a *chassid* and I wish to do more than the law requires."

There is no substitute for a competent Torah authority to serve as a mentor. This means that we must be ready to yield to a higher authority when it conflicts with our own judgment. This requires *mesiras nefesh.*

The Primacy of Middos

Conventional wisdom is that Torah teaches us character development and how to refine our traits. This is certainly true, and you can therefore imagine my astonishment when I came across this comment by the great ethicist Rabbi Yerucham Levovitz (in italics, no less): "Torah and wisdom are *not* the remedy for objectionable traits, but just the reverse. When we refine our *middos,* only then do we acquire Torah, and this is the truth." (*Da'as Chochmah U'Mussar,* Volume 4, Page 96.) In other words, one cannot rely on Torah to initiate *middos,* but *middos* must precede Torah.

I really should not have been shocked by this statement, because the Talmud says, "Proper behavior must precede Torah"

(*Vayikra Rabbah* 9:3). Yet the emphasis that Rabbi Levovitz puts on this is most impressive. One cannot begin to benefit from Torah unless one has made himself into a suitable receptacle to receive it.

Rabbi Levovitz cites a verse from the Scripture, where Moses admonished the Israelites: "You have rejected G–d Who is in your midst" (*Numbers* 11:20), upon which Rashi comments, "If not that G–d's presence was among you, you never would have had the audacity to act this way." Rabbi Levovitz points out that the immanent Divine presence among the Israelites not only did not deter them from acting improperly, but to the contrary, it contributed to their misbehavior. Precisely because they felt they were so special, so unique, their vanity caused them to disobey G–d. Rabbi Levovitz associates this with a Talmudic observation about Torah: "If one is deserving, Torah becomes a life-sustaining medicine. If one is not deserving, Torah can be a deadly poison" (*Yoma* 72b).

There are many fine character traits which one should acquire, and there are traits of which we should divest ourselves. There is a rule of thumb that can help us identify the nature of our traits. The Talmud says, "When G–d wished to give the Torah to Israel, He could not find *anything* that could contain it for them other than *shalom* (peace)" (*Uktzin* 3:12). The wording of this Talmudic statement is significant. It is not that *shalom* is just conducive to acquisition of Torah, but that it is the single essential factor that makes acquisition of Torah possible. The Talmud refers to *shalom* as the only vessel that can contain Torah. Clearly if this vessel is defective, it is like pouring water into a container that has a hole in the bottom, and the water will flow out just as it flows in. Similarly, if our *shalom* is defective, we have no way of retaining the Torah we may acquire.

The traits that are preparatory for Torah are those conducive to *shalom*: to be kind, to be considerate, to help others, to avoid embarrassing anyone, to forgive, to apologize, to restrain one's anger, to avoid speaking or listening to *lashon hara*, to give *tzedakah*, etc. Obviously, behaving contrary to these traits, which would undermine *shalom*, will result not only in failure to absorb Torah, but what is even worse, rendering the Torah we do learn toxic.

No one would stop off at a *treifah* (non-kosher) fast food outlet on the way to a Talmud *shiur* (lecture), yet it is not unthinkable that one might listen to some gossip or even speak disparagingly about others prior to a *shiur*. Rabbi Levovitz says that this undermines our capacity to benefit from a Torah *shiur*. Rabbi Yisrael of Salant cites the case of a person who is hurrying to a *shiur*, and is so determined to get there in time that he behaves rudely and pushes people out of his way. Better that he would have stayed home, say our ethicists. Torah thus acquired while our *middos* are defective is useless at best, and harmful at worst.

We would be less than truthful if we asserted that we are sufficiently diligent in all the traits that are conducive to *shalom*. To develop them to their fullest, we would have to put forth significant effort, perhaps even to the degree that constitutes *mesiras nefesh*. But let us not deceive ourself. Without this *mesiras nefesh* for *middos*, all our efforts at Torah may be in vain.

We are now better able to understand the declaration *Naaseh v'nishma,* "We shall do and we shall listen," with which the Israelites accepted the Torah at Sinai. The obvious question is: How can one do before one hears what one is supposed to do? How can there be a *naaseh* before *nishma*? Rabbi Levovitz's exposition clarifies this. *Naaseh* refers to activation of proper character traits, which the Talmud says we would have been obligated to implement even if the Torah had not been given to us (*Eruvin* 100b). Our ancestors correctly grasped this principle, and this is why they were able to receive the Torah. This is why they were able to be in perfect unity at Sinai (*Exodus* 19:2), having divested themselves of those traits that undermine *shalom*.

As we have noted, the declaration of the *Shema* represents the concept of *mesiras nefesh*, and again, not necessarily the *mesiras nefesh* of martyrdom, but a *living mesiras nefesh*. The Talmud states that the *Shema* is divided into several portions, the first being "accepting the sovereignty of G–d" and following this, the performance of mitzvos. The order cannot be reversed.

The first portion of the *Shema* contains the paragraph *ve'ahavta,* and we have seen that this means not only to love G–d, but also to make His Name beloved (*Yoma* 86a). This can only be accomplished by incorporating those traits which we have cited as promoting *shalom*. It is then and only then that we can move on to the rest of *Shema*, which instructs us to learn Torah, to teach Torah, and to perform mitzvos.

Let me digress here to observe that the principle which I have extracted from the works of *mussar* have just recently been introduced into the psychologic profession, and constitute a near-revolution from traditional psychology. It had previously been assumed that in order to help a person overcome symptoms of an emotional disorder, he must attain a thorough understanding of their origin, such as what happened in his formative years that led to the development of his emotional problems. This is the *nishma* component. Modern psychology, which has been influenced by behavioristic philosophy, has taken the approach of changing unhealthy behavior first, and dealing with its origins later. It took psychology a long time to realize what our ancestors knew 3,000 years ago, that *naaseh* must precede *nishma*.

The great ethicist, Rabbi Yisrael of Salant, said that it would have been easy for him to compose complex works on *halachah* comparable to the monumental works of the *Noda b'Yehudah,* "But I could not compose even a single page of *Mesilas Yesharim (Path of the Just)*." A person may be born with the capacity of being an intellectual genius, and it is relatively simple for him to acquire encyclopedic knowledge, but transforming one's inborn traits to become a spiritual person is a Herculean task, even for someone who is born an intellectual genius.

The interdependence of *shalom* and *middos* is clear. What is less clear is how something which is so crucial and vital to Torah and to our very survival can be so ignored and abused. The *Midrash* states that when Jerusalem was destroyed and its inhabitants massacred, the heavenly angels complained to G–d that this decree of punishment was far in excess of His own guidelines, to which G–d responded, "But there was no *shalom* among them." Think of it! We bewail the terrible tragedies that have befallen our people throughout history, yet the *Midrash* states that these could all have been avoided if only there had been *shalom* among us. Let us realize that when we refine our *middos* and thereby enhance *shalom*, we are not only making ourselves into better people, not only enabling ourselves to acquire and retain Torah, but are actually contributing to our very survival and warding off great harm to our people. We earn greater Divine protection by developing *middos*, and even if it takes *mesiras nefesh* to do this, it is much to our own advantage.

The Absolute Goal

This chapter is essentially theoretical, because we may assume that the absolute goal is probably beyond reach of most if not all of us. Nevertheless, it is well to know what the ultimate goal is, because perhaps if we aim for the stars we will reach the moon. If we only aim for something close to us, we may never advance at all.

Two chassidim were once engaged in a discussion. The first said, "What is your goal in life?" The second answered, "My goal is to be as great as the Baal Shem Tov."

"That is an impossibility," the first said. "My goal is to be a good chassid."

The second chassid shook his head. "If you aspire to be

as great as the Baal Shem Tov," he said, "you may end up being a good chassid. If you only aspire to be a good chassid, you may end up being less than an average Jew."

Thus, even if absolute perfection is beyond our reach, we should nevertheless know what it consists of.

The Torah says that we are "to love G–d, to listen to His voice, and be attached to Him, for He is your life" (*Deuteronomy* 30:20). The ultimate in "attachment" is to be totally absorbed within G–d Himself.

The Talmud states that the relationship of a *tzaddik* before G–d is similar to that of a candle before a torch. If you approximate a candle to the flame of a torch, you will note that the larger flame attracts the small flame of the candle, even to the point where the flame of the candle may jump and be absorbed into the larger flame. So it is with the *neshamah,* which is part of G–d Himself, and the craving of the *neshamah* is to rejoin with G–d and be absorbed into Him, rather than being separated and enclosed within the human body, which constitutes a physical barrier between the *neshamah* and G–d.

It is certainly commendable for a person to have a strong craving for a closeness to G–d. However, if we analyze this closely, we see that a craving for closeness with G–d presupposes two components in a relationship: the person and G–d. Just as there can be undesirable cravings which the person has, there can be commendable cravings, and the desire to be close to G–d is certainly highly commendable. Nevertheless, in order for there to be a craving, there must be someone who craves. A *total* self-effacement and a *total* absorption into G–d essentially eliminates the ego of one who craves. It is, as it were, as though the person goes out of existence, and is entirely absorbed within the Almighty.

*I*t *is related that someone discovered Rabbi Schneur Zalman in a state of devotion, exclaiming with every bit* *of energy, "Master of the universe! I do not want Your Gan Eden (Paradise). I do not want Your Olam Haba (World to Come). I want only You."*

The question is: Is it possible for a human being to achieve such a state of absorption and still remain in existence? If the ultimate is that there not be a person who craves, because one has been totally absorbed into G–d, can one then continue to exist as a live person?

Some of the commentaries explain the phenomenon of the death of Nadav and Avihu, the two sons of the High Priest, Aaron, using precisely this theory. These two highly spiritual people achieved a state of such extreme closeness to G–d that their *neshamah* left them (*Leviticus* 10:1-2; 16:1).

The Rabbi of Gur gave the following explanation: It is indeed possible for a person to achieve so intense a devotion with the performance of a mitzvah that his *neshamah* leaves him and joins its source in the Almighty. However, since it is G–d's wish that the person continue to function and perform mitzvos, G–d designed the mitzvos in such a manner that they would sustain the person's life even when he achieved an intense closeness, and it is this unique feature of the mitzvah that prevents the *neshamah* from leaving the person. As the Torah relates, Nadav and Avihu performed a service that they had not been instructed to do. Hence, the protection of a mitzvah was not available to prevent their *neshamah* from departing from them. This is why their approaching G–d resulted in their death.

We can now better understand the structure of the verse that we mentioned earlier, "To love G–d, to listen to His voice, to cleave to Him." It is the fact that we "listen to His voice," in other words perform the mitzvos which G–d has instructed us, that provides the possibility of having so intense a love for G–d that we cleave unto Him and become absorbed in Him, yet are able to remain alive.

Earlier we noted that the term *mesiras nefesh* was not accurate, since it was not the *nefesh* or *neshamah* that was being surrendered, but rather the *guf.* In this absolute devotion to G–d, there is literally a *mesiras nefesh,* since we turned over the soul itself to G–d, and it is only by virtue of the unique lifesustaining feature of the mitzvah that our *neshamah* remains with us and we continue to function as living human beings.

Although this intense *mesiras nefesh* may be beyond our reach, it is well to be aware of it, if only that we should not be content with the degree of spirituality we may have reached. It is possible for a person who is totally committed to Torah and mitzvos to feel that he has achieved the ultimate in spirituality. It is well to know that there is still a higher degree of spirituality for which we should strive.

Epilogue: A New Automaticity

Towards the very end of my writing this book I came across a number of essays by the great ethicist, Rabbi Yerucham Levovitz, in *Da'as Chochmah U'Mussar*, Volume 4, which validate my thesis. What I have been referring to as constituting a *living mesiras nefesh* is nothing other than improving one's character and developing oneself spiritually. Rabbi Levovitz says that this is a challenge which indeed requires an intensity of effort that can only be termed *mesiras nefesh*. Let me cite excerpts from these essays.

The Torah tells us of the intense fear the Patriarch Jacob had of his brother Esau, and that when an encounter with him was unavoidable, Jacob sent a lavish gift and messages of appeasement. Ramban says that all these methods were essential because Jacob did not wish to rely on some miraculous change of Esau's feelings toward him.

But why would such a change require a miracle? Rabbi Levovitz asks. Is it that uncommon for a person who pleads for compassion and mercy to be forgiven? Granted that Jacob had offended Esau by taking his father's blessings from him, but is it not possible that even without a miracle, Esau, who had now become wealthy and successful would forgive his brother for an event that occurred so many years ago?

Rabbi Levovitz concludes that when an emotion such as hatred takes root in a person's heart, it takes a miracle to totally extirpate it. Furthermore, the fact that Jacob had experienced miracles, such as his crossing over the Jordan River with only his staff (*Rashi, Genesis* 32:11), still did not reassure him. The uprooting of a deeply ingrained emotion is a greater phenomenon than any other supernatural event.

Rabbi Levovitz cites a *Midrash* which states that when Joseph revealed his identity to his brothers, their first impulse was to kill him. Even though they appear to have sincerely repented their cruelty toward him, and felt that the ordeal they were being put through in Egypt was a Divine punishment for having sold Joseph into slavery (*Genesis* 42:21-22), their hatred was nevertheless rekindled when they discovered that he was the viceroy. This indicates to us how difficult it is to totally rid oneself of an objectionable emotion, and that traces of it may remain even when one thinks he has overcome it. This is why nothing less than an intensity of *mesiras nefesh* will suffice to change one's character traits.

The chassidic master of Rizhin once saw a young man who was fasting and engaging in other self-flagellation. "Just what are you trying to do?" the Rebbe asked. "I am trying to break some of my undesirable character traits," the young man answered. The Rebbe said, "You will break your neck before you succeed in breaking any character traits with your method. The Talmud says that the only antidote to the yetzer hara is Torah (Kiddushin 30b). If you will learn Torah, do the mitzvos, and pray to Hashem to remove your objectionable character traits, you will succeed."

You will recall that the *Zohar* refers to Torah as the "blueprint" according to which G–d created the world. The *yetzer hara* is a natural instinct, a group of impulses that are inborn and are natural to man. The only way these can be modified is by the method contained within the blueprint of nature, the Torah. In order for this to be achieved, Torah must be studied properly, and not for ulterior motives, and both Torah study and performance of mitzvos must be done with the intent that they bring about the salutary changes in character. Rote study and performance will not accomplish this.

We can now see the direction in which we have been progressing. You will recall Rabbi Dessler's description of the struggle with the *yetzer hara* being a battlefield, with an active front where the actual fighting goes on, and an area which had already been conquered and is secure and in which there is no longer any struggle. Rabbi Dessler states that spiritual progress consists of advancing the front and making more and more areas secure and battle free. In other words, more and more things are no longer subject to the struggle of *bechirah* (free choice); just as the person who is sincerely committed to eating kosher and has done so all his life does not even have to give any thought to passing by a cheeseburger stand. Rejection of *treifah* food has become *automatic.*

Earlier we spoke critically of operating on automatic and stated that one must avoid habit and operate on manual. This is indeed true, but if we extend Rabbi Dessler's principle to its logical conclusion, it is to arrive at a new automaticity, to so develop ourselves spiritually that we have no desire other than to do the Divine will.

This ideal state occurred at only two points in history, the first being in *Gan Eden* before Adam's sin.

Rambam asks: How is it that after the sin in Eden, Adam acquired the capacity to distinguish between good and evil? It would appear that this is hardly a trait which should be the consequence of a sin. Rambam goes on to explain that before the sin, Adam was in so pristine a spiritual state that he instinctively would have avoided any improper behavior. Just as an animal instinctively avoids eating poisonous plants, so Adam had an instinctual repulsion of anything evil. As a consequence of his sin, Adam lost this spiritual status, and now had to rely on intellect to rationally analyze and distinguish between good and evil, right and wrong. It is clear that instinct is far superior to rational deliberation, so that the acquisition of the ability to intellectually distinguish between right and wrong which replaced the intuitive distinction was a loss and a demotion in spirituality rather than an advancement.

The second point in history occurred when the Israelites received the Torah at Sinai, and they returned to the pristine state of *Gan Eden* prior to the sin. They lost this precious state with the worship of the golden calf. (The obvious question, how could Adam and the Israelites commit sin at all when they were in so pristine a state, is dealt with at length by Torah commentaries.)

Whereas it is unrealistic to aspire to a spiritual state as lofty as Adam's before the sin, we nevertheless should retain it as the ideal. Even if we cannot possibly develop an instinctual avoidance of wrong, we can advance the battlefront so that more and more things are automatically repelled, which will then free up our energies to triumph in those areas where the struggle is ongoing. Very few of us can realistically aspire to be among the top 10 wealthiest people on earth, yet this does not hinder us from trying to increase our material wealth. Our attitude toward spiritual wealth should be no different.

Living mesiras nefesh may appear to be a tall order, and one might think it is beyond reach. Moses anticipated this, and after instructing us to be totally devoted to G–d with all our heart and soul (*Deuteronomy* 30:10), he tells us that it is not beyond reach, not in the heavens, nor across the ocean, but very close to us, that we may achieve it (ibid 30:13).

We can feel secure that Moses was right, and if it appears to us to be beyond our reach, this is only the *yetzer hara's* way of trying to frighten us, to discourage us from doing what is well within our means. Indeed, we must only try, only make a beginning, and we are assured of G–d's help in bringing our striving to a successful conclusion: "Give Me an opening like the point of a needle and I shall open for you a portal wide enough to allow chariots to pass through" (*Shir HaShirim Rabbah* 5:3) We need only initiate the process, but we must do so with sincerity and with the desire to reach the goal.

This volume is part of
THE ARTSCROLL SERIES®
an ongoing project of
translations, commentaries and expositions
on Scripture, Mishnah, Talmud, Halachah,
liturgy, history, the classic Rabbinic writings,
biographies, and thought.

For a brochure of current publications
visit your local Hebrew bookseller
or contact the publisher:

Mesorah Publications, ltd.

4401 Second Avenue
Brooklyn, New York 11232
(718) 921-9000